Traditional
Shirred &
Standing Wool
Rugs

OTHER TITLES BY THE AUTHOR

Rugmaker's Handbook Series:
#1 Knitted Rag Rugs for the Craftsman
#2 Fabulous Rag Rugs from Simple Frames
#3 Crocheted & Fabric Tapestry Rugs
#4 Traditional Shirred & Standing Wool Rugs

Other titles:
Bohemian Braid Rugs for the Beginner
Multi-strand Braids for Flat-Braided Rugs
Flat Wrap Rugs and Baskets
Introduction to Patched Rugs
Amish Knot Rugs
Broomstick Rugs
Chain Braid Rugs
Wagon Wheel Rugs
Anchored Loop Rugs (American Locker Hooking with Rags)
Bodkin Rugs
Introduction to Tambour Rugs
Knotted Shag Rugs
Pjonging and the Single Strand Chain Braids
"Hook Braided" Rugs; the Two-strand Attached Chain Braid
Kitchen Table Rugs
String Crochet Rugs
Primitive Rug Hooking, An Introduction
"Beaded" Rugs, A Unique Standing Wool Rug
A Rugmaker's Sampler

Rugmaker's Handbook No. 4

Traditional
Shirred &
Standing Wool Rugs

Third Edition

written and illustrated by,
Master Rugmaker
Diana Blake Gray

Rafter-four Designs
Cocolalla, Idaho

Rugmaker's Handbook No. 4
Traditional Shirred & Standing Wool Rugs
Third Edition

Rafter-four Designs

For information address:
Rafter-four Designs
P O Box 40
Cocolalla, ID 83813
http://www.rugmakershomestead.com

including information from:
Traditional Shirred & Standing Wool Rugs, 1st Ed.
copyright 1988 by Diana Blake Gray
Traditional Shirred & Standing Wool Rugs, 2nd Ed.
copyright 1996 by Diana Blake Gray

ISBN: 1-931426-31-7

Printed in the United States of America

PREFACE

I am often asked what I mean by "traditional" rag rugs. My definition is that traditional rug techniques are those that were passed hand-to-hand, from one rug maker to the next. Though a few types of rag rugs were made in Europe, the vast majority of the techniques evolved in North America and, because of the cultural dynamics of the 19th and 20th centuries, most of those same techniques were also simply forgotten when they stopped being passed down.

Understanding how that happened, is a study in shifting populations. (I'll be describing the United States, but the same process occurred in Canada.) During the 19th century, the vast majority of Americans lived in rural, isolated areas. Transportation and communication were slow and in frontier areas, farms, ranches and communities were, by necessity, as self-sufficient as possible. The principle of "waste not, want not" was simply a part of their way of life.

Isolation did not stymie inventiveness and creativity however. The plethora of rug making methods that developed during those days was the result of the settlers' desire to use everything, combined with the desire to create something both beautiful and practical. Girls were schooled in a wide variety of needlework from an early age so the skills necessary to create rag rugs were widespread. It should not be surprising that in that type of environment so many different types of rugs were made. And once someone discovered a practical technique, it was passed along much as favorite recipes were shared.

By contrast, the Industrial revolution led to larger and larger concentrations of people in eastern cities, and in the last half of the 19th century improvements in printing made the production of mass market publications affordable to city dwellers. Ladies magazines appeared—first for the more affluent like Godey's Ladies Book—and then for the middle class. The magazines became both a means to disseminate information and arbiters of what sort of information was worthy of publication. "Fine needlework" was the order of the day and "rag" rugs were largely ignored. These city-based publications regarded themselves as too sophisticated for plebian rural skills, concentrating on the "fashionable" instead. Even by the early 20th century, books were being written to try to stem the tide of losing these rural skills, but only a very few found a market. (Amy Mali Hicks' "The Craft of Hand-Made Rugs," published in 1914, was a notable exception, but it should be noted that even she made an effort to cover the subject, shirred rugs were not included, likely because by that time they were largely forgotten.)

In the second half of the 20th century, the population of the US became dominantly urban, and rural traditions and practices were less and less valued. In the case of most of the rag rug techniques, it took only one generation for a rug method to fall out of use completely. Even to this day I hear the same story: "My grandmother made this rug, but my mother didn't, and I wasn't interested when I was a kid. Now grandma is gone and I don't know how to do it."

There were a few exceptions to this pattern of course. Loom woven rugs, hooked rugs and 3-strand braided rugs continued, as well as a few others. The one common factor among the surviving methods was that they had a commercial value of some kind. Businesses were built providing rug looms, rug hooks and printed patterns, braiding cones and wool, and various sorts of rug making gadgets. But for those rug making methods that didn't require a special tool or material, there was no economic incentive to preserve the method and no cultural imperative to keep the tradition alive. Indeed, the making of "plain" rag rugs was generally disdained, being regarded as something only the poor did.

I find it fascinating that now, in the first decade of the 21st century, we have come full circle. The frontier principle of "waste not, want not" has been reborn in the desire to recycle to lessen our impacts on the planet. What began for me as an effort to document, pass along, and indeed celebrate, the creativity of pioneer ancestors, has become

PART 2:
HANDBOOK FOR SHIRRED & STANDING WOOL RUGS
> Threads
> Needles and Hooks
> Fabrics
> Estimating Yardage
> General Guidelines for Fabric Preparation
> A Quick Guide to Strip Width
> Cutting Knit Fabrics
> Cutting Felted and Similar Non-Woven Fabrics
> Cutting Woven Fabrics
> When Cutting on the Bias
> Fabric Appearance
> Usaing Multiple Strips and
>> Combining Different Weights of Fabric
> How to Recycle Common Types of Clothing for Rugs
> Recycling T-shirts and Sweatshirts
> Recycling Cotton or Synthetic Sweaters
> Recycling Socks
> Recycling Old Jeans
> Sculpting the Edge of a Shirred or Standing Wool Rug
> Creating Special Design Effects with Sculpting
> Repairing a Hole in a Shirred Rug
> Making Your Own Non-Skid Mat
> Caring for a Shirred or Standing Wool Rug
> Hanging Shirred or Standing Wool Rugs for Display

Questions I get asked

How do I cover up mistakes in stitching?
Can I Use Wool Blends?
How Big of a Rug Will a Sweater Make?
Can I Use Cotton Yarn with Cotton Sweaters?
Can I Do Edge Shirring with Recycled Sweaters?
How Do I Make THAT Rug?
How Much Can I Sell a Shirred Rug For?
Are These Rugs Suitable for Children?
Are Crochet-Shirred rugs Better than Sewn-Shirred Rugs?
Where Can I Find Affordable Wool for Beaded Rugs?
Can I Use Lining Material for Shirred Rugs?
Why Should My Rug Lay Flat?

Acknowledgements

This book would have been a lesser project were it not for the thousands of rug makers who have asked questions over the past twenty one years since the publication of my first book on shirred and standing wool rugs. In particular, a thanks to my students who always know to ask the questions that I don't know the answers to. You keep me on my toes.

INTRODUCTION

The process of gathering fabric along a thread was used in antiquity, for both practical and decorative textiles. In rug making, the term "shirring" appears to have been applied to any rugs made by gathering since at least the mid-19th century. In sewing, the term shirring refers to using two or more parallel threads, but no one was being particular in describing rugs that used only a single thread for gathering fabric strip into folds.

True shirred rugs are completely made of shirred fabric with the shirred sections joined together to form the (reversible) rug. Some confusion has crept in because various authors have identified rugs as shirred rugs, when they really are not. When fabrics are gathered and then stitched to a base fabric, they belong to the family of "sewn shag rugs" rather than shirred rugs. Typical of this group is the "caterpillar" rugs of the 19th century in which a center-sewn shirred strip was sewn to a base fabric (ticking, duck or canvas).

Similarly, standing wool rugs are made solely of edge-set fabric strips and are reversible. Rugs where wool strips are sewn side-by-side to a base fabric also belong to the family of "sewn shag rugs."

From existing examples, it isn't clear whether standing wool rugs preceded shirred rugs, since they appear in the same decade (1870-1880) but logic would presume that the simpler standing wool construction came first. Standing wool rugs have remained as a sewn rug construction virtually unchanged. Shirred rugs are a different story.

Early shirred rugs are all sewn (center-shirred or edge-shirred). By the 1890s examples occur where the shirred sections were made with a crochet chain, and then the chains sewn together (see the "Snow-on-the-Mountain" rug).

Around 1900 crocheted shirring was being done on slightly recurved afghan hooks (thus the "bent hook" term) and the chain shirred sections were being joined by crochet stitches also. Within 20 years, special crochet hooks were being marketed just for these rugs.

Because the processes of creating shirred rugs and standing wool rugs are so basic, the equipment used to make them is also of the very simplest nature. Thus, in trying to market tools for making these rugs in the twentieth century, an important aspect has been to give the tool an exotic name and avoid the simpler terms.

Some of the various gadgets for making shirred and standing wool rugs that have been marketed include:

—For the bent hook style of crocheted shirring, there have been the "Art Rug Needle," the "Shirret" ™ hook, the "Rugbee Rug Needle", the "Schirren" hook and others of similar design.

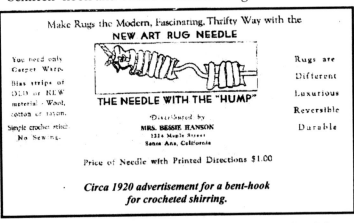

Circa 1920 advertisement for a bent-hook for crocheted shirring.

Several manufacturers including the Art Rug Needles (hooks) were marketed as a home business for women who learned to make the rugs, and then sold hooks and taught rug making to their friends. Similar marketing schemes were used for many household products of that period.

—For standing wool rugs, a wire wheel was marketed as the "Palm Loom," where strips of wool were wrapped around the wheel and then stitched through. Below is a photograph of a "Palm Loom" and a rug shown in their advertisements.

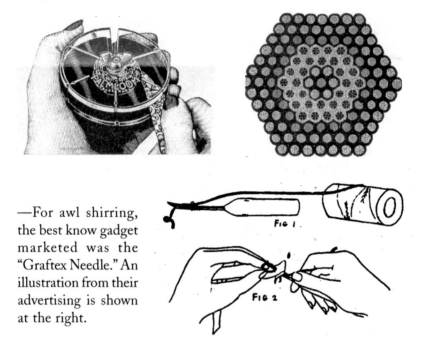

—For awl shirring, the best know gadget marketed was the "Graftex Needle." An illustration from their advertising is shown at the right.

A perusal of women's or needlework magazines from 1910 through 1950 reveals that these and other rug making gadgets were quite well-promoted and apparently widely used. Today, however, very few of these tools are recognized unless they are still with their original instructions or packaging.

Gadgets may seem an amusing sidebar to the history of shirred and standing wool rugs, but they shouldn't be dismissed lightly. Without the entrepreneurs marketing their wares, these varieties of rugs would have been forgotten as so many others have. For example, the simplest type of center sewn shirred rugs had pretty well disappeared by the 1920s because the technique only required a plain sewing needle (eliminating the opportunity to market a "special" tool for it). So the center-sewn shirred rugs vanished, while the more elaborate methods with "special " tools survived in various forms.

CHAPTER 1

THE BASICS

Shirred and standing wool rugs are some of the most interesting and richly textured of the handmade rugs. The fabric is used sideways so that the edges are exposed, and packed solidly to give the rug both body and softness. There are also variations of standing wool rugs constructed to appear as if they are shirred. Those methods are called faux shirring. Finally, there are rugs that are made from a single piece of fabric gathered along many threads to form the rug. Following is a general guide to the main types.

Standing wool rugs are constructed by laying wool strips side-by-side and stitching them into solid unit. A standing wool rug does not have as much "springiness" as a shirrred rug, especially when made of the traditional heavy woolens. Standing wool rugs can be very exciting visually, and this technique can be combined with other shirred methods to make exquisite rugs or hangings.

A plain standing wool rug (above) has strips of fabric laid side-by-side. At left is the "beaded rug" variety of standing wool, composed of very small pieces of fabric.

TOOLS, FABRICS & THREADS

The only tools needed to make a standing wool rug are a cutting tool (scissors or a rotary cutter) and a fairly long needle. Almost any embroidery needle can be used, but a little more needle length is desired. A long, soft-sculpture type of needle is ideal because it has a fairly large eye and is up to five inches long.

The easiest fabrics to use for standing wool rugs are thick, heavy fabrics with a lot of body. As the name implies, the traditional fabric was heavy wool. Some modern fabrics will also work such as polar fleece or heavy acrylic blanket fabric. You can also use lighter fabrics for this technique by using several layers at a time. See the Handbook section for more information about using multiple strips.

You can use any of the threads for stitching that are discussed in "The Basics", but my preference for wool rugs is 2- or 3- ply linen. Linen is sometimes difficult to find (and is relatively expensive) so a good mercerized crochet cotton is a good second choice.

For your first standing wool rug, you can recycle a thick blanket (it doesn't have to be a wool blanket), or a sweater or coat. The basic directions are for a blanket, but in the Handbook section, you'll find directions for recycling other items that you may have on hand.

For the sample rug I'm using an old acrylic blanket, which was not only worn and tattered, but had also been washed with another fabric that left dark pills all over the light colored blanket.

Even though the blanket is pretty much past being presentable as a bed covering, it will make a very attractive rug since it will only be the edges that are visible.

Start by cutting the hems and selvage edges off of the blanket, then cut 12 to 15 inches off one end. From that piece you will cut bias strips for the rugs.

The "bias" of a fabric is the diagonal. The strips should be 1/2 to 3/4 inches wide if you are making a rug. Strips of any width can be used for wall hangings. Trim the ends of the strips so that they are square. (If you are using fleece, a felted wool or melton wool the strips can be cut on the straight grain.) There is more information about cutting on the bias in the Handbook section.

Once the strips are cut, you're ready to begin constructing sewing the rug together. Always work on a flat surface when making a standing wool rug. If you want to work sitting on the couch use a lap board. Card tables are a good height for working and large enough to be able to see that the rug is laying flat as you stitch.

Thread the needle, double the thread and knot it securely. Remember that it is the thread that holds the rug together, so always use a doubled length of thread.

To Start a Round Standing Wool Rug

Coil a wool strip snugly to make a round about 1-1/2 inches across. Stitch through the center five or six times. Each stitch should pass through the center of the coil and come out on the other side.

To Start an Oval Standing Wool Rug

Fold a wool strip to the length of the center of the rug. Fold it again over the beginning end of the strip. Stitch through the three layers from one end

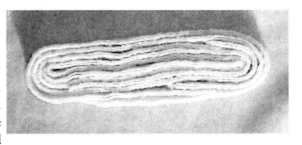

to the other, working toward the loose end of the strip. Stitches should not be more than 1/2 inch apart.

Stitching Together a Standing Wool Rug

The stitching pattern for a standing wool rug is the same no matter what shape you are making. The needle is inserted at the outside of the rug and angles upward. It should emerge at least three layers in.

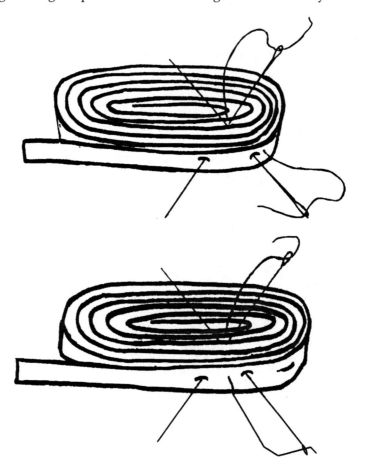

Then insert the needle in the same place that the thread emerges between the layers of wool, pointing toward the outside edge. The needle should come out about 1/2 to 1 inch away from the last stitch. (The closer you place your stitches, the stronger the rug structure will be.)

When you reach the end of a fabric strip, lay the end of the next strip so that the ends just touch, and continue sewing. When the end of the thread is reached, knot it off and begin a new thread, going over the last stitch again. You want the stitches to be firm, but don't pull on the thread so hard that it distorts the fabric.

As you stitch the rug, make sure that the top and bottom edges of the strip line up with the previous rounds. Minor variations in strip width are unavoidable, and they add textural interest to the rug. It is really important to work on a flat surface to keep the rug flat and the edges as even as possible.

The rug gets larger by continuing around and sewing more strips. You can finish off a standing wool project at any point. Around the outer edge, make the stitches a little differently than you did for the rug. Insert the needle in the same place that the thread comes out on the edge, angling the needle toward the next stitch. The thread will sink into the wool, but the stitch won't pull out. At the very end, hide the final knot in the thread between rows of strip.

You will notice that as you make your stitches, the strip will have a slight tendency to pucker. Do not force the strip to absolute flatness. The bit of pucker lets the rug surface have a little give and increases the softness of the rug. Also if you force the strip flat the rug will have a tendency to cup.

Working Spirals

I used to be adamant about not sewing on more than one strip at a time. However, you can sew two or three strips at once if you make your stitches deeper. The needle should penetrate at least five layers into the rug. This is how a simple spiral is made.

Select two contrasting strips to use together, and start and sew the rug as usual. You can use light and dark strips of the same color or two different colors, and the strips do not all have to be the same colors so long as there is a contrast between them. You treat the two strips just as if they were a single strip, always keeping the dark and the light fabrics in the same relative positions.

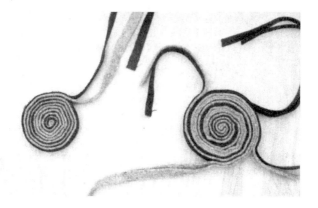

More complex spirals can be made by working several pairs of strips in sequence. You will need a separate needle and thread for each pair of strips. Stitch one pair until it "catches up" with the next pair, then switch to another pair. These complex spirals are most effective if each pair has one light strip and one dark strip.

Multiple Centers

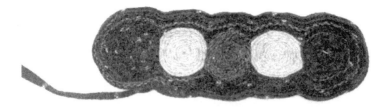

One of the most striking standing wool rug effects is created by working many different centers. Usually these are small round centers, but they can be of almost any shape. Make sure to stitch the centers together solidly, and have at least two complete rounds of bordering strip around them.

Small round centers can be assembled in straight rows as shown above, or in a staggered pattern. Freeform shapes can be assembled in any configuration. Below is a set of five centers stitched in a curve.

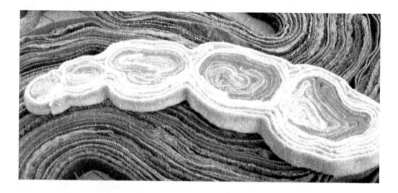

These examples have the multiple centers stitched together so they act as a single unit when the rug is constructed. Rounds of standing wool strips are stitched continuously or in lines, framing the multiple centers.

A different approach to multiple centers in standing wool rugs is to create small pieces that are placed throughout the rug or wall hanging. They centers each become mini-rugs that are bordered with standing wool and the mini-rugs are then stitched together, forming the finished rug. When using multiple centers in this way, voids are created where the mini-rugs don't fit perfectly together, and those voids need to be

filled with small sections or pieces of standing wool.

In the photograph, the freeform centers are shown in a layout with lines of standing wool around them. Note the voids that would need to be filled with additional wool strip. These centers were actually used for the

Islands in the Stream freeform rug discussed next, and are shown here simply as an illustration of separated multiple centers.

Freeform Shapes

The basic traditional standing wool rug is worked in a continuous spiral, but it is not necessary to always do this. The strip can be worked back and forth to create any shape for a design in the rug. Also, remember that rugs do not have to be round or oval. You can make a rug in any shape. Rugs with irregular shapes are real eye catchers.

Because of the way standing wool strips appear, it is best to choose a design for the rug that is strongly linear. The lines can follow any shape to outline or emphasize a feature. The sketch here shows multiple centers arranged for a floral effect. If your design can be sketched in continuous lines, it is a good one for a standing wool rug.

Another approach to freeform rugs are designs that are based around many parallel strips of standing wool. For example a tree trunk can be assembled from a center of several strips which open up at the ends.

By folding the strips back and forth, greater textural depth can be created as in the photo at right.

Small motifs can be inserted between the linear standing wool strips--a technique that would be used to placed leaves on the tree, for example.

Whether constructed from single center or multiple centers, a freeform rug is the most fun of any of the standing wool rugs, because it will continually surprise you as you work. Following is a case study of one.

Islands in the Stream:
A case study in a freeform standing wool rug.

The concept for this rug was to take advantage of the linear form of standing wool to represent flowing water. I began by cutting ¾-inch strips from all sorts of shades of blue, turquoise, green and gray. Then I laid the strips out next to each other in random order.

Because there were so many strips, I stitched lines of basting thread through the whole lot, about three inches apart, just to keep them from moving around while I decided on the ultimate arrangement for them.

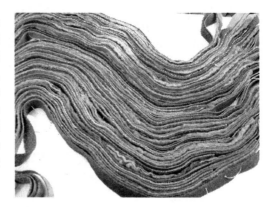

Next, I stitched five small freeform centers, in graduated sizes to represent islands. At this point, I wasn't sure whether I wanted the islands to remain separate or be a unit.

Because the strips forming the "water" were basted on long threads, I could move them back and forth to play with different layouts. One of the test layouts is shown on the previously, with the islands spread around on the base.

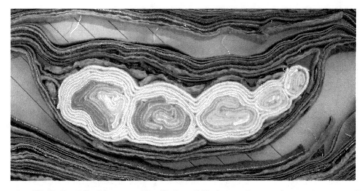

Eventually, I decided to use the "islands" as a unit, so they were stitched together and bordered with a light blue. Note in the photo that there were small spaces between the "islands" which were filled with short sections of the light blue strip.

Once the center island unit was complete, I began to stitch the bordering strips of "water" around the island unit. Because I wanted the lines of "water" to flow around the islands, small pieces of wool were also added at each end of the island unit, as shown below.

From that point on, the wool strips representing the water were stitched layer by layer around the outer edge to form the rug. The design (while not quite what I originally envisioned) is a good example of how the linear nature of standing wool works to create motion in a rug, and would work just as well to depict a sky in a landscape design.

Once the basic shape of the rug was complete, several rounds of standing wool completed the border. The black and white image emphasizes the textures of the different types of wool in the rug, and the finished rug is shown in color on the back cover.

Islands in the Stream

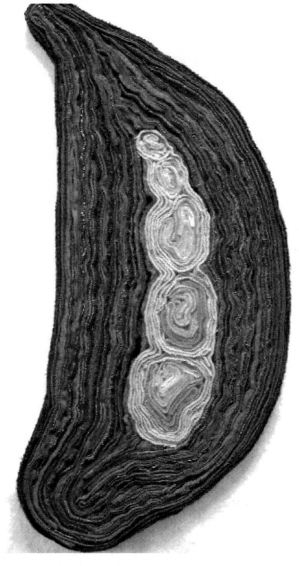

CHAPTER 3

BEADED WOOL RUGS

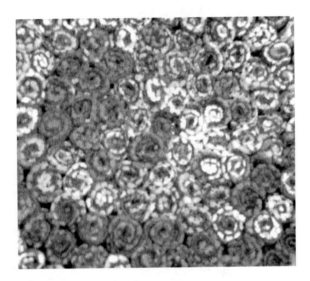

Beaded rugs are one of the most interesting of the standing wool rugs, since they can be worked as a textile mosaic. Each bead becomes a point of color, allowing for transitions of shades within a design or a distinct line, so the possibilities for rug design are virtually limitless.

Most often these rugs were made without a design plan, in a hit-or-miss style, resulting in a rich blending of tones, and no distinct lines. Because beaded rugs were made with very small pieces of heavy wool, they could be made with the pieces of scrap which were too small for any other application. Typically, these scraps were from wool used for overcoats, either when the coat was first cut out, or in making over the coat for a different use. Old examples also survive that were made with leftover felt from millinery.

Beaded rugs are reversible, with the same pattern and texture on each side, and are quite durable when constructed properly.

Fabrics for Beaded Rugs

Unlike many of the other techniques in this book, there is really only one sort of fabric that works well with beaded rugs and that is a **thick wool**, either fabric or felt. Blanket wool is ideal. Coat wool can be washed and dried hot to shrink it to the proper thickness and old wool sweaters can be likewise washed and dried to shrink. (All recycled fabrics should be cleaned before cutting.)

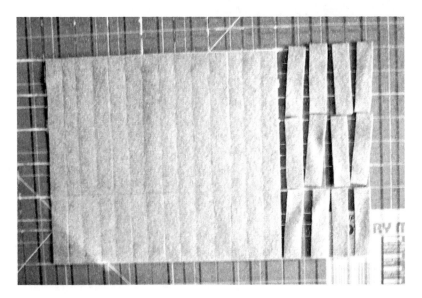

The pieces for beaded wool rugs should be cut ¾-inch wide and 3 inches long. The most efficient way to cut the pieces is with a rotary cutter and mat, as shown above. Note that there are cutting lines drawn directly on the mat at 3/4-inch intervals. Of course sewing shears will also do the job. If using scissors, the most efficient procedure is to cut the fabric into 3-inch strips and then cut the 3/4-pieces from that. For most of the heavy wool, the direction of cutting makes no difference since the surfaces are at least partially felted to preven ravelling.

Ideally, all of the wool in the rug should be of the same heavy weight so that the beads are of the same diameter. However, you can also include "beads" made with slightly lighter wool fabrics, if you cut them longer so that they roll up to the same diameter as the heavy wool.

The beaded rugs with the richest appearance are made with wool that has at least two different colors in the weaves. Twills, plaids and patterned wool are ideal.

Solid color wool can appear to leap off the rug and even in dark colors will stand out from the patterned wools. In the photos notice how solid colors appear more prominent while the multicolor wool beads tend to blend together.

General Directions for Beaded Rugs

Beaded rugs can be (and usually were made) as a two-step process, as they are the easiest to make. First the beads are strung, then the strings of beads are sewn together to form the rug. (Another, less often used method, which makes beaded rugs in a single step is include later in the chapter. It is a bit more complex, but is the most adaptable for the textile artist who wants to create a rug with elaborate designs.)

TWO-STEP METHOD FOR BEADED RUGS

Rolling & Stringing the Beads: Cut a section of thread about 5 or 6 feet long. Thread the needle and knot the thread so that it is doubled. Select one piece of wool (3/4" X 3") and roll it from one end to form the bead.

The easiest and quickest way to roll the beads is to place a piece of wool lengthwise in the palm of your left hand. Slide the palm of your right hand down (toward the fingers). You will feel the wool roll up under your hand. Left-handers use the opposite hands.

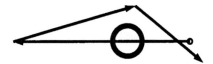

Insert the needle through the bead and slide it down the thread. Insert the needle between the threads next to the knot, and pull up the thread. This will secure the first bead so that it can't slide off the end of the thread. (Note that in the stitching diagrams each circle represents one rolled "bead" of wool. The arrows show the direction and sequence of stitching.)

Roll another piece of wool into a bead and insert the needle through it. Always insert the  needle into the "tail flap" of the bead so it stays rolled up. Slide the bead down the thread. Repeat with the next piece of wool and the next. (I make put several beads on the needle before sliding them down—it goes faster.)

The beads should fit snugly against each other, but don't cram them together so that their round shape is distorted.

When the end of the thread is near, take a second stitch going back through the last two or three beads, and knot the thread securely. Thread the needle with another doubled section of thread. Pass the needle back and forth through the last bead strung, catch the knot with the needle, and proceed with stringing more beads. When you have several feet of beads strung together, you can start assembling the rug. It is best not to let the beaded string get too long, because it will get tangled and is a mess to unsnarl.

Assembling a Rug in Rows

A square or rectangular beaded rug can be made by working in rows, back and forth, with the strung beads. The beads can line up from row to row, or be offset, just so that there are the same number of beads in each row. Note that you will be able to move the beads a little along the strings to make sure their placement is where you want.

Thread the needle with a doubled length of thread, and knot securely. The rug is stitched together, bead by bead, going into the previous row of beads. Take one stitch going through the current bead into the previous row.

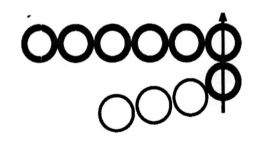

Then make a stitch coming back out through the next bead. Repeat the process for each bead along the string until you reach the end of the row. Then stitch the next row the same way.

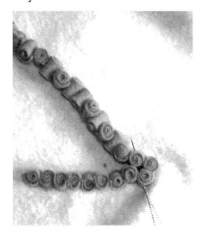

Assembling a Coiled Rug

A round or oval bead rug is made by coiling the strung beads in the desired shape. For a round rug, begin with the first 7 beads, coiled toform a small circle. Thread the needle with a doubled length of thread, and knot securely.

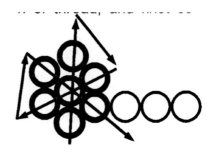

Stitch back and forth all of the way through the circle several times, making sure each bead is stitched.

Then working around this center in a spiral, stitch each bead to a bead in the previous round as follows.

Take one stitch going through the current bead into the previous row.

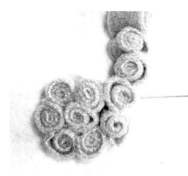

Then stitch back through the same bead angled to the next bead in the center.

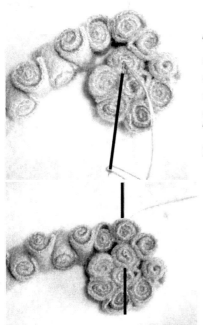

Then insert the needle into the same place that the thread comes out and make a stitch coming out through the next bead around the outside, and repeat the process. The dark line shows the needle position.

Note that this is a different procedure than used to create the center. Each bead is stitched to the rug individually, and by using this method, the stitches at the outsisde of the rug are hidden Take deep stitches that penetrate the next row of beading. Work on a flat surface to keep the rug flat.

You want your stitches to be quite firm, but not so tight as to distort the beads or the rug. After you have sewn two or three rounds of beads, look at the edge of the rug. If you notice that the edges tend to cup slightly, that means your stitches are too tight. Your rug should be laying flat to the table by itself.

Then, pull gently on the sides of the rug center while looking through it. The rug should have a little give, but not much. There also shouldn't be any noticeably larger gaps between some of the beads. If there are, that means your stitching is just a little too loose or it is uneven (some tight and some slack stitches). It takes a little practice to get the feel of the proper thread tension for beaded rugs.

Continue stitching the beads to the rug in a continuous spiral. As it gets larger, periodically check that there aren't any gaps where a bead was missed in the stitching. If you find one, start a new thread and reinforce that spot with a couple of stitches. (You'll need to bend the rug upwards slightly.)

To Begin an Oval Beaded Rug
String several feet of beads, and begin the center by folding over a section of beads. The folded section should be equal to the length minus the width of the finished rug size.

Begin at the fold, stitching each pair of beads together.

When you reach the end of the center section, curve the strung beads around it and continue stitching just as described for the round rug.

Work around the center in a continuous spiral. When you run out of doubled thread, tie it off securely and start a new section with the first stitch going twice through the last bead sewn. Keep the knots hidden between the beads.

SINGLE STEP VARIATION

For the textile artist, there is the option of a one-step assembly of beaded rugs. This has the advantage of more precise placement of particular colors for a design. Generally for a precisely planned design, it is good to have worked out the color placement on a sheet of graph paper, with each square representing one bead. The main design is worked back and forth, row by row, following the chart. Then a border of continuous strands can be added.

First row.

Double and knot the thread. String the first bead, pushing it down to the knot. Place a second stitch going all of the way through the bead, securing it in place. String the second bead, pushing it down the string in place next to the first bead.

Continue stringing beads until you have the correct number for the base row of your design. Make sure that the beads are snug together, but not packed tightly.

Second row. String one bead, and take a second stitch through it. The second stitch through each bead keeps it from moving on the string.

Finish the first bead of the second row with a stitch going through it, pointed toward the second bead.

String the second bead, and stitch it to the matching bead in the first row.

Finish stitching the second bead with a stitch pointed toward the third bead. Stitch the third bead in the same way as the second, and continue along until you reach the end of the second row.

Following Rows

String the first bead, pushing it along the thread until it is in place. It should align with one other bead. Take a second stitch through the bead to hold it in place along the string.

Then stitch through the bead it lines up with, going all of the way through that bead. Reverse the stitch and come back out through the new bead. Angle the stitches going in and out so that the thread doesn't pull back out. Run the needle through the new bead again so that the thread is lined up, ready for the next bead in the design.

Repeat this process with each bead across the row, and with all following rows until the design is complete. Note that there will be threads that show on the ends of each row. Make a border of at least one row of continuous beads to hide these.

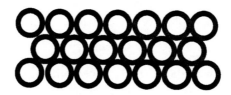

Offset Rows, How to Stitch

Beads in off-set rows will make a tighter structure for the rug, but are more difficult to plan into a design since the lines aren't straight. For off-set rows, use designs with diagonal lines.

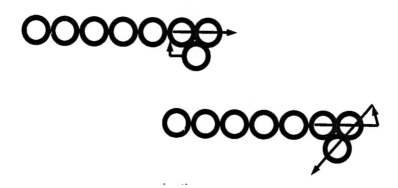

String a line of beads for the base row of the rug. When beginning the second row, the first bead is placed along the string so that it lies between the last and the next to last bead in the base row. Stitch into the next-to-last bead of the base row, and through the last bead in that row.

Then angle the needle so that the next stitch passes through the new bead and so that the thread comes out ready for the second bead in the row. The triangular stitching continues across the row. Note that there will be one less bead in the second row than there was in the base row.

For the third row, stitch one bead only to the last bead in the second row. Then proceed to place the beads between the beads in the second row.

End the third row with one bead placed outside the last bead in the second row. Continue adding rows: one "long" and one "short" alternately for the entire length of the rug. If you notice a distortion in your design (usually caused by using beads of different diameters), you can correct it by adding a small "filler" bead to an indented area, or using a half-size bead in an over-full area.

When the design area is completed, border the rug with continuous rounds of beading to hide the stitches at the ends of the rows.

Milleflore Beaded Rugs

These beaded rugs are made by assembling many uniform round centers to create an overall effect similar to the glass *milleflore* beads. Each center is composed of concentric rows of one color.

The colors for *milleflore* centers can be uniform throughout or they can be wildly mixed, resulting in a rug that resembes a hexagonal pieced quilt like Grandmother's Flower Garden.

The technique is expandable to entire rugs, assembling one round of beading at a time for concentric rows of color throughout. By counting beads in the whole-rug plan, design motifs can also be added. The milleflore method combines elements of both one-step and two-step beaded rugs, so there is a lot of freedom for design.

Milleflore centers should be made of three rounds of wool beads for easiest assembly of the rug. Pull off about two yards of thread, thread the needle, and knot the thread ends. Make a loop around the first bead on the string by passing the needle back through the knot.

To create a 3-color milleflore center, string **one bead** for the center, then **six beads** for the first round of color, followed by **twelve beads** for the third round. Do not knot off the string. Cut the thread near the needle, but do not knot the thread yet. To create an evenly spaced milleflore center, you may need to move the beads along the string or even add or remove a bead at the end.

Re-thread the needle with a single length (knot only on one thread end) using about a yard and a half of thread. Pass the needle through the center bead and into the third bead on the string.

Arrange the six beads of the first color evenly around the center bead, and stitch through each bead passing through the center bead with each stitch. (This is the same as the beginning of any round beaded rug, diagrammed previously.) End the stitching with the needle comin out of the center bead.

Arrange the twelve beads of the outer color around the edge so they are spaced evenly and just touch at the end of the circle. You may need to adjust the position of the beads along the string or even remove a bead or rethread the needle and add another bead. (That's why the string holding the beads together isn't knotted off until the last bead in the third row is stitched to the center.)

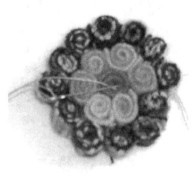

Stitch from the center out to the last bead on the string to hold it in place. Then knot off the thread holding the beads together.

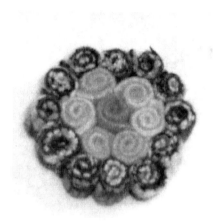

Work around the outside, stitching each bead individually to the center, ending with a stitch through the first bead. End off the thread with a knot or a back stitch. The milleflore center should be generally round with distinct rows of color. If it isn't perfect, don't worry too much, since there will also be distortion of the shapes when the individual pieces are stitch together.

When you have at least seven individual units completed, you can begin to assemble your rug. Round rugs are created by selecting one unit as the center, and surrounding it with six others (just like the center of the beaded piece).

At the left is a center, laid out, but not sewn. (Notice that all of the milleflores are still round.)

Compare it with the photo on the next page of the sewn-together center and note how the rounds get altered to a hexagonal shape when they are put together snugly.

If you are planning a large rug, especially one with an intricate pattern, complete all of the individual units and safety-pin them together to make sure of your layout.

For long runners, squares or rectangles, begin by assembling the individual pieces in offset rows.

To assemble the pieces into a rug, select the center and one other milleflore. Using a doubled length of thread, stitch through the edges of each piece with deep stitches. You will need to lift the work off of the surface to do the stitching.

Each stitch will begin in one mille flore and end in the other, coming out on the top side. (Stitch the whole rug from the same side.)

Notice that the center motif has 12 beads around the outside and will be joined to six other pieces.

Ideally, each of the outer pieces should touch two of the beads in the center motif, but since there will be variation use that as a guideline rather than an absolute.

The next piece will be stitched both to the center and the previous piece, and each succeeding piece will be stitched the same way.

Notice that the motifs form three lines going through the center. If you keep the idea in mind that the motif should line up with its opposite, you stitching will result in a reasonably round center.

The rest of the rug is assembled in the same fashion. Each milleflore unit will be stitched to two others. For a round rug, keep adding pieces around the outside of the center in concentric rows. For any other shape, just make sure that each motif is stitched to two others, fitting between them.

At the outside edge, you may want to form a more regular line. Three, four or five beads are stitched into the "notches" formed by the milleflore units to fill in the gap. You will have to adjust at each notch to accomodate it, since each one will be a little different. You can border the rug with a solid line of beading or two if you like, stitching each bead so that the outside stitch is not noticeable. (Insert the needle in the same place the thread comes out, but angle the needle in a different direction. That will allow the thread to bury itself in the wool and be invisible.)

Larger Milleflore Units and Rugs

Individual milleflore units can be made larger, but as the size increases, they will not fit together neatly and the gaps where three units meet will need to be filled in with individual beads.

To create a 4-color milleflore center, string **one center bead**, then **six beads** of the second color, **twelve beads** of the third color and finally **eighteen beads** for the fourth color.

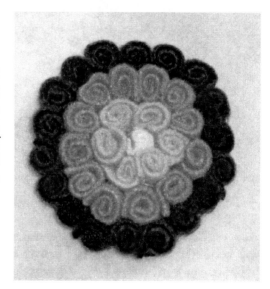

Then follow the directions for a 3-color center, continuing for a fourth row, and don't knot off the thread until you have stitched the fourth color. (You may want to create it in two steps if you are using beads of different weights, since the number in the third round may need to be adjusted.)

Milleflore centers can be made larger if desired. Each round of color will have six more beads than the previous round if all of the beads are of the same diameter. The problem with making milleflore centers larger than four rounds is that when they are assembled, the larger units may not have sufficient "give" to form the hexagons that let the units fit snugly together. The larger the centers, the more likely that there will be gaps between them. The voids can be filled with more wool beads.

To make an entire rug with concentric colors, begin with a three-color milleflore center. Then string beads for each round on a doubled thread. Stitch each row to the center as it is completed, fitting it exactly to the rug center. Make sure that each bead is individually stitched.

CARING FOR A BEADED WOOL RUG

A wool beaded rug is not fragile, but should be handled with respect. Try not to pick up the rug by the edge which places all of the rug's weight on just a few stitches. Instead, roll or bunch the rug up to move it around, especially if it is a large rug.

Vacuum regularly with the suction attachment only, making sure to vacuum both sides. For stain removal use a mild product designed for wool. If the rug needs thorough cleaning, have it professionally dry cleaned, don't use water since the rug will get very heavy when wet and the stitching can stretch.

Rug cleaning machines can also be used with the suction only attachment (no rotating brushes), but be sure that the rug is completely free of soap residue and thoroughly dry before using the rug.

Likewise, to store the rug, never fold it since the pressure at the fold can stretch the stitching. Instead, store it flat or roll it up loosely over a cardboard tube or around another rolled rug.

CHAPTER 4

SEWN FAUX SHIRRING

There are three ways to make a "faux" shirred rug. (Rugs that look like shirred rugs, and act like shirred rugs, but aren't really shirred rugs.) The first method is the most basic, using just a needle and thread. The second and third methods create identical rug structures but use different tools and reversed techniques. Both create loops of thread, that secure the folds of the faux shirring, but one is done with a small crochet hook and the other with an awl. Once either of these two are completed, it is impossible to tell which method was used to make the rug.

For the beginner, the sewing method of faux shirring is the easiest. However, the folds won't be perfectly uniform or evenly spaced. That usually isn't a problem since most of the sewn faux shirred rugs are made for utility and comfort. Most often (and most practical) is to turn an old blanket into a soft bedside rug. (These feel marvelous underfoot.)

For more elaborate faux shirring projects, I will admit to being biased in favor of the crocheted faux shirring, simply because it is easy to do, and lends itself to creating designs in the rug. By comparison, "Awl" faux shirring is awkward and time consuming. In the mid-twentieth century, the awl technique was promoted by the Graftex Company as a way to market their particular tool (a scaled down awl they called a "texing needle") so examples of that technique are not uncommon.

Sewn Faux Shirring

Sewn faux shirring is really a modification of the standing wool technique, but rugs made this way look like they have been shirred. If you look closely at "real" shirred rugs the folds all radiate out from the center. In faux shirred rugs the folds lay flat around the rug. Essentially, the rows are a piece of standing wool with bends formed at regular intervals.

Sewn faux shirring works best with relatively heavy fabrics with a lot of body, such as heavy wool or acrylic blankets or fleece fabrics. You can also use this technique to recycle heavy sweaters or socks. (See the Handbook section for how to prepare those for rug making.) The rugs are springy and soft underfoot, and feel very luxurious. Faux shirred rugs can be made in almost any shape, even freeform rugs just like the standing wool rugs.

You can mix a lot of colors in a faux shirred rug without fear that they will clash. Small wool or blanket remnants, or a mix of heavy socks or sweaters work great for these rugs. Use solid colors in several rows to create a line in the design. For more subtle transitions of colors use plaids, prints or twills for a gradual color change from row to row.

Use a good quality mercerized cotton crochet thread for these rugs or 3-ply linen for all-wool rugs. A long embroidery needle or soft sculpture needle is used to sew the rug together. (The longer the needle, the deeper the stitches you will make and the stronger the finished rug will be.)

For most woven materials, strips for the rugs should be cut 3/4 of an inch wide but for supersoft bedside rugs using old blankets or sweaters strips cut one inch wide make rugs with a more luxurious feel.

Directions:
Cut the fabric strips on the bias, to the desired thickness of the rug. (In the photo, a veteran blanket with a large floral print was used. The strips were cut one inch wide.)

The directions say to pinch a half-inch fold with each stitch. That will make the strongest rug since the stitches will be closer together. However, feel free to ignore the directions. You can pinch folds of one inch or even longer as long as you sew the folds down about every half-inch. (In the photo series, folds are about one inch.) The appearance of the rug isn't affected by the size of the folds, but it is by how evenly the folds are made, so find a size you like and stick to it.

Always work on a flat surface, either a table top or a lap board. Thread the needle with a double length of the thread and knot the end.

ROUND RUGS WITH SEWN FAUX SHIRRING

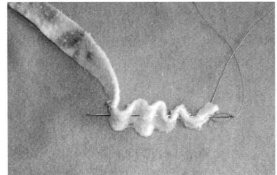

Work the needle in
and out of the strip
five or six times to
make a short
gathered section.

Coil this section to a round
shape
 and make several stitches
through
 it to secure it.

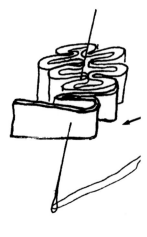

Pinch a half-inch fold in the strip with your left hand and hold it against the center of the rug. Insert the needle into the center of the rug slanting upwards so that the needle comes out in the center.

Insert the needle back into the fold so that it comes out to the edge of the rug again.

Then pinch another fold and repeat the process. (Note that it doesn't make any difference whether you sew clockwise or counter-clockwise.)

That's all there is to it. You just work continuously around the outside of the rug pinching folds and stitching them down.

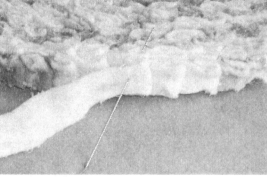

Your stitches should be firm, but don't pull the thread too tight or it will distort the shape of the rug.

When you come to the end of your thread, just knot it so that the knot doesn't show, and start with a new length of thread. When you come to the end of a fabric strip, pinch the next fold from a new strip.

OVAL RUGS WITH SEWN FAUX SHIRRING

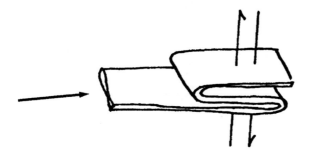

Use a doubled length of thread. Make a 1/2 inch fold in a fabric strip, and insert the needle into it, then back up.

Pinch another fold of the strip, and stitch in and out of it the same way. Continue pinching folds until the center section is as long as you'd like.

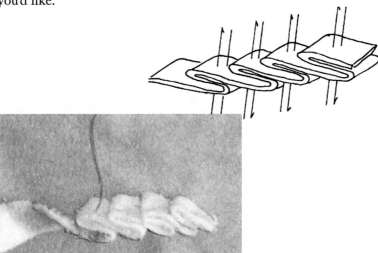

Fold the strip around the end of the center, pinch another fold and stitch it.

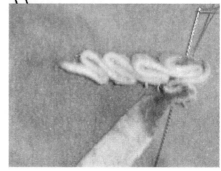

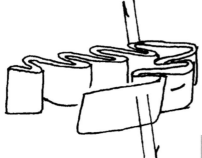

Pinch a second fold, stitch down, and repeat along the side of the rug. At the other end, pinch folds to work around the curve, stitching as you go.

Then just follow the basic directions for sewn faux shirring. When your rug is of the size that you want, stop shirring on a curved area so that the change shows the least.

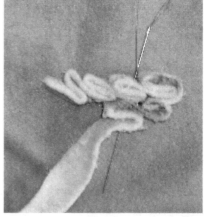

CHAPTER 5

FAUX SHIRRING
WITH A CROCHET HOOK

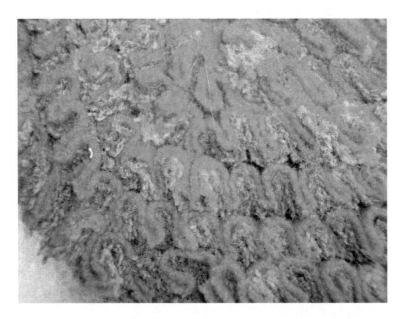

Of all of the faux shirring methods, this is my favorite. It is
fairly simple to learn and makes for good lap work. You don't
have to count folds to work in a pattern or count rows to work
increases. In other words, once you learn the basic stitch, you
really don't have to think about this method while you work, so
it becomes quite relaxing.

The only thing to keep in mind with this method is that the crochet thread will show at the outside edge of the rug. This can be overcome in two ways. First, you can select a thread color that closely matches the color of the fabric you are using so that the thread is less obvious at the edge. Second, you can add a final row of center-sewn shirring or crocheted shirring as a border.

Crocheted faux shirring works best with medium weight fabrics like skirt weight wool. That's not to say that it can't be done with other fabrics, because you can use knits (even t-shirts) and heavier fabrics. However, the tip of the crochet hook has to be able to penetrate the fabric without struggle so test your chosen fabric and thread with various sizes of steel crochet hooks. Don't mix weights of fabric in a single rug since the resulting crochet stitches will be of different sizes. (For the photos, I'm using a coat weight melton wool simply because it photographs more plainly. Once you learn the method, you can also use two strips together as was done in the rug in the photo on the previous page.)

Usually a size 5 to size 8 hook works the best. Very open-weave fabrics may allow for a slightly larger hook while denser fabrics will need a smaller hook. Unlike crocheting with yarn only, the hook itself doesn't determine the stitch size. Instead, the stitch size is created by the bulk of the fabric you use. As long as you choose a hook that will handle the type of thread you are using, it will work fine for rug making.

Woven fabrics should be cut it into bias strips ¾ inch wide for most rugs. Light fabrics can be cut up to one inch since the fabric will compress and the strip width will be a little less than the thickness of the rug. Clip the ends of the strips so that they are square. (See the Handbook section for how to cut knit fabrics.)

Use a good quality mercerized cotton crochet thread like DMC Baroque cotton or a heavy-duty upholstery thread. Do not use 4-ply cotton thread sold as "rug warp" since it doesn't have the tensile strength needed for a good, strong rug. Keep in mind that these rugs are held together only by the thread used for crocheting, and if you can easily break the thread by pulling on it, the rug can be "broken" just as easily.

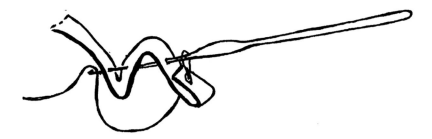

The basic stitch used with the steel hook method is to insert the hook down through the fabric strip, up through the fabric strip and then down again.

This is followed by completing a chain stitch with the thread (as you begin the rug) or with a single crochet stitch in the body of the rug. Keep your crochet stitches relaxed, the top loop of the crochet stitch will be fairly large since it covers a complete fold of fabric. If the loop "sinks" into the fold or the fold buckles, your stitch is too tight.

When you get to the end of a fabric strip, just start the next. For instance if you can go 'down' and 'up' through the fabric strip and come to the end, just start the next strip of fabric by inserting the needle for the final 'down'. (You will find yourself saying "down, up, down" with each stitch, but just explain to anyone who complains that the book says its is OK to talk to yourself.)

Crocheted faux shirring can be worked back and forth in rows or formed into a round, oval, square or rectangle. Any shape that can be done with a single crochet stitch can be made with crocheted faux shirring, so once you have the basics mastered, don't feel constrained by the patterns given here. Between the ease of making designs and the shapes possible, this is an excellent method for the textile explorer.

Crocheted Faux Shirring Back and Forth in Rows

This is the simplest of the crocheted faux shirring patterns and is a good place for a beginner to start. Have a few strips of fabric ready and we'll begin with a small sample so you can get the feel of the stitching. Once you've completed a small sample, you're ready for a rug project.

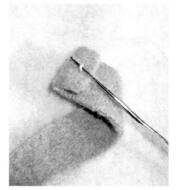

1. Insert the hook into a fold of the fabric strip. Place a slip knot on the hook and draw it up through the fabric on the hook. The hook and the loop will end up on the top of the fabric strip, and the thread underneath the strip.

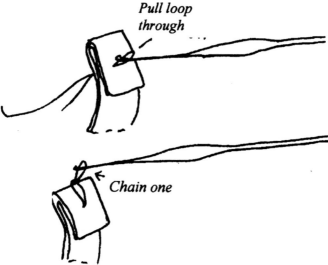

Pull loop through

Chain one

Then Chain 1and turn the work so that the hook is pointed toward the fold.

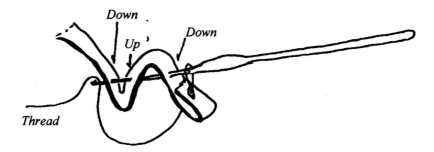

2. Insert the hook into the fabric strip going down, then coming up from underneath and finally going down through the strip again. Draw up a loop of thread through the fabric strip, and complete the chain stitch with the loop already on the hook. Repeat this until you have ten or twelve complete repetitions.

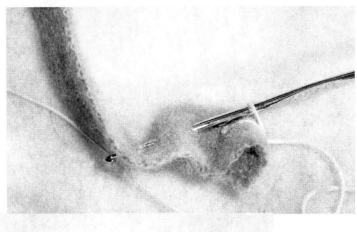

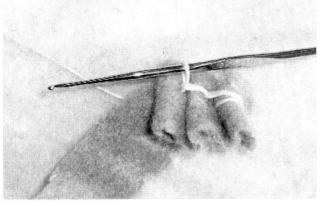

When the first row of your sample is stitched, you'll have extra strip left. In order to turn the work and crochet the next row, the end of the fabric strip needs to be trimmed off. Cut it about 1/4 inch (or half a fold). Then chain one with the thread.

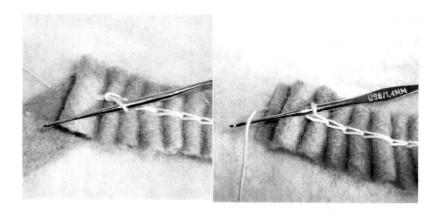

Turn the piece around so you can work back for the next row. Have the chain stitch on the hook, and with a new piece of fabric strip, take the hook down, up, down through it.

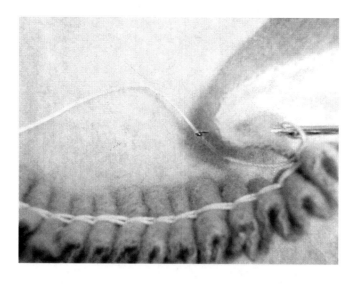

Look at the crocheted chain, and notice there is one loop of thread over every fold of fabric. The single crochet stitches for this row will be placed under both threads on the folds. Since they really are chain stitches, we'll call them one stitch. You'll be making one single crochet stitch in each of the chain stitches on the firsst row, except for the very first one.

Skip the first set of threads. Insert the hook under the next chain stitch, draw up a loop (two loops on the hook)

Yarn over the hook, and pull a loop through both of the loops on the hook. Note this is just a single crochet stitch.

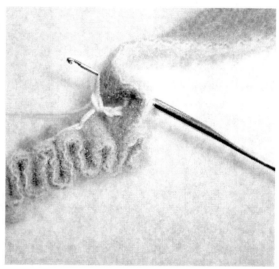

Now, pull the loop of thread that is on the hook through the folds and the last loop.

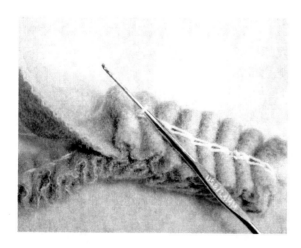

Repeat the process: Down, up, down through the strip, one single crochet under the next chain stitch; one single crochet; pull thread through the folds and the final loop.

When you reach the end of the row, clip off the fabric strip. Then chain one and turn the work. Repeat the process for the second row, where you skip the first set of threads and then alternate putting folds on the hook with a single crochet stitch.

Make two three more practice rows and then it's time to try switching colors in a row so you can see how easy it is to make patterns with this technique.

At any place along the row, clip the fabric strip after you've completed a single crochet. Leave a little bit of fabric past the stitch. Work across you sample changing from one fabric to the next every two or

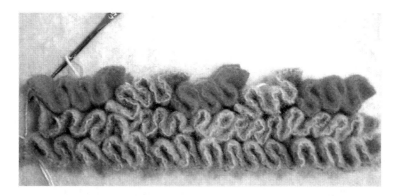

three stitches. That's all there is to it. Finish your sample by practicing the stitching (and more color changes) for a few more rows until you feel comfortable with the process. To end off, finish any row, make one chain stitch, clip the thread a few inches away and bring it up through the chain stitch. Use an embroidery needle to work the thread end back into the rug.

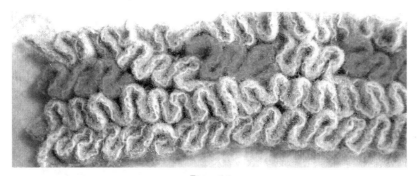

TO START A ROUND OR SQUARE

1. Insert the hook into a fold of the fabric strip. Place a slip knot on the hook and draw it up through the fabric on the hook. The hook and the loop will end up on the top of the fabric strip, and the thread underneath the strip.

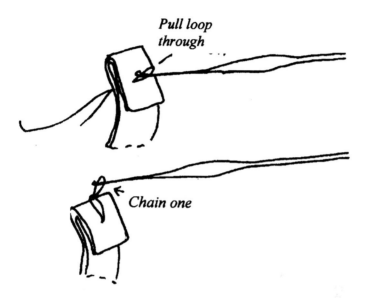

Pull loop through

Chain one

Then Chain 1and turn the work so that the hook is pointed toward the fold.

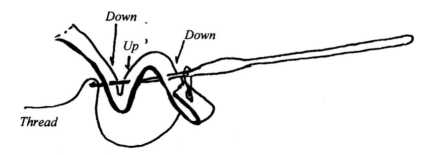

Down

Up

Down

Thread

2. Insert the hook into the fabric strip going down, then coming up from underneath and finally going down through the strip again. Draw up a loop of thread through the fabric strip, and complete the chain stitch with the loop already on the hook. Repeat this until you have six complete repetitions.

Page 55

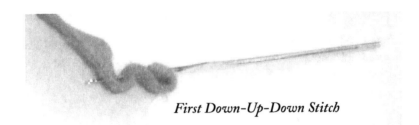

First Down–Up–Down Stitch

Thread over hook...

Pull loop through folds

Pull loop through folds

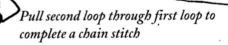

Pull second loop through first loop to complete a chain stitch

Repeat a total of six times

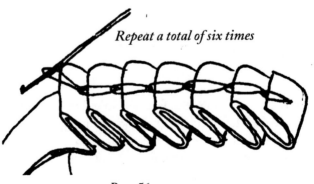

Look at the shirred strip. On the top of the strip you will see two threads for each stitch, on the underneath side you will only see one thread for each stitch. All future stitches will be worked on the two-thread side.

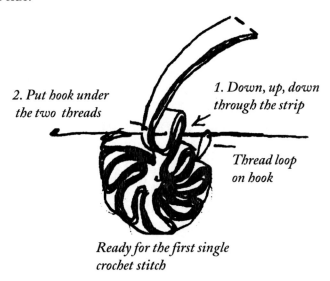

2. Put hook under the two threads

1. Down, up, down through the strip

Thread loop on hook

Ready for the first single crochet stitch

3. Insert the hook into the fabric: down, up, down. Roll the section of folds into a tight coil so that the two-thread side is visible. Insert the crochet hook under the first two-thread stitch. Draw a loop of thread underneath the two-thread stitch. Pull a second loop of thread through the loop on the tip of the hook, then pull this same loop through the fabric folds and through the loop of thread on the hook.

Page 57

Note: This stitch is just a Single Crochet. The only difference from what you are used to is that you work it through some fabric folds just before the stitch is finished. Mark this first stitch with a small safety pin so you will know where the row begins and ends.

4. In this first round of single crochet stitches, you will place **two** complete stitches under each of the two-thread loops of the center. Each stitch is made by inserting the hook (down, up, down) through the fabric strip, then making a single crochet under the two-thread loop. As you complete the single crochet, work the loop through the fabric folds.

In this first round of crocheting, you will have six pairs of single crochet stitches (12 stitches in all). Peek between the folds to count stitches.

CONTINUING A ROUND SHAPE

The crocheting continues in a spiral, do not chain up between rounds. In the second full round you will also place two single crochet stitches in each space (a total of 24 stitches in the round.)

The round shape is continued by placing six pairs of stitches evenly around each row of crocheted faux shirring. Only one crochet stitch is made in all of the other two-thread loops. I use six small safety pins to mark the placement of the paired stitches.

CONTINUING A SQUARE SHAPE

With the completion of the first round, make sure that you have 12 two-thread loops showing at the outside edge.
Second round: *Work three single crochets (with the fabric strip on each one) in the first two-thread space. Then work one single crochet in each of the next two spaces. * Repeat the * sequence three more times, and mark each of the four corners with a safety pin. The corners of a square are made by placing **three** single crochet stitches in the two-thread loop at each corner.

TO START AN OVAL OR RECTANGLE

Both the oval and rectangle are begun with a long faux shirred section. The length of this section is determined by taking the desired finished length of the rug and subtracting the finished width. For example if you want to have a finished rug that is 5 feet long and 3 feet wide, you will begin with a shirred section that is 2 feet long (5 - 3 = 2).

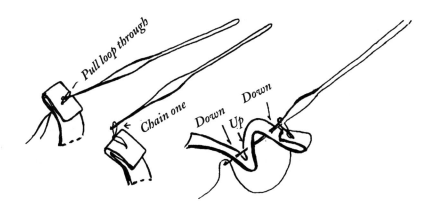

1. Insert the hook into a fold of the fabric strip. Place a slip knot on the hook and draw it up through the fabric on the hook. The hook and the loop will end up on the top of the fabric strip, and the thread underneath the strip. Then Chain 1 and turn the work so the hook faces the strip.

2. Insert the hook into the fabric strip going down through the strip, then up and down again. Draw up a loop of thread through the fabric strip, and complete the chain stitch with the loop already on the hook.

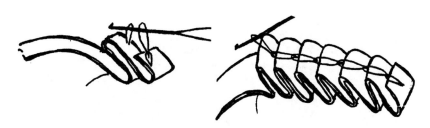

Repeat this until the shirred section is the desired size for the center of your finished rug.

Look at the shirred strip. On the top of the strip you will see two threads for each stitch, on the underneath side you will only see one thread for each stitch. Fold over the end of the shirred strip so that you can place your next stitch on the side that has only **one** thread showing for each stitch.

3. Insert the hook into the fabric: down, up, down. Skip the first single-thread space and insert the crochet hook under the next single-thread. Draw a loop of thread. Draw a second loop of thread through the loop on the tip of the hook, then pull this same loop through the fabric folds and through the loop of thread on the hook.

Note: This stitch is just a single crochet. The only difference from what you are used to is that you work it through some fabric folds just before the stitch is finished. Mark this first stitch with a small safety pin so you will know where the row begins and ends.

4. Each stitch is made by inserting the hook (down, up, down) through the fabric strip, then making a single crochet under the single-thread. As you complete the single crochet, work the thread loop through the fabric folds.

Continue along the single-thread side inserting one single crochet in each space until you reach the end of the faux shirred section. In the very last space again insert three single crochet.

5. Turn the end of the work so that the double-thread loops of the center face you. In the first space work **three** single crochets. Then work one single crochet in each space until you reach the last space, and there again work **three** single crochets.

CONTINUING THE RECTANGULAR SHAPE

The work proceeds in a spiral, do not chain up between rounds. At all four corners you will be placing **three** single crochet stitches in one space. Place a safety pin at each corner to remind yourself. Everywhere else only one single crochet stitch is placed in each space.

CONTINUING THE OVAL SHAPE

The work proceeds in a spiral, do not chain up between rounds. In order to make the oval rug lay flat each round of single crochet stitches must have additional stitches.

At both ends of the oval you will need to place three pairs of crochet stitches, evenly placed. This is easiest to do if you put three safety pins at each end of the oval. Whenever you reach a safety pin, make two single crochet stitches in the same space. Everywhere else only one single crochet stitch is placed in each space.

MAKING A PATTERN OR DESIGN

This type of crocheted faux shirring lets you create elaborate patterns and designs. You can change fabric color with every stitch if you want. When you are ready to change colors, simply clip off the strip that you want to end and start with the next color.

For a small spot of color cut a strip to 1 to 1.5 inches long and use it for only one down-up-down sequence.

Use a piece of graph paper and colored pencils to chart elaborate designs just as for cross stitch. (In fact you can use some simple counted cross stitch patterns, but the patterns will be slightly distorted since the stitches in the rug aren't perfectly square.)

CHAPTER 6

FAUX SHIRRING WITH AN AWL

Awl shirring is traditionally done with a standard leather-working awl. There have been several patented devices (such as a "texing" needle) which were developed to make this form of faux shirring a bit less chancy. The directions here are for a standard awl or punch needle, but can be used with any similar device.

PARTS OF A TYPICAL AWL

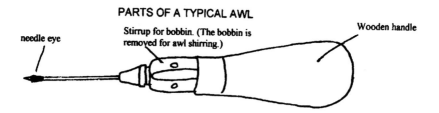

needle eye — Stirrup for bobbin. (The bobbin is removed for awl shirring.) — Wooden handle

A standard leather-working awl is about eight inches long, but the special awls made just for rug making are only about half as long, to fit easily in the palm of the hand.

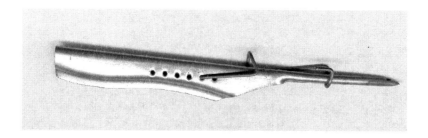

All of these specialty awls included a depth gauge to create uniform loops. In the photo, the depth gauge is adjustable. While unmarked, this old awl is not one of the Graftex "texing" needles since they incorporated a curve at the tip.

CHAPTER 7

SEWN CENTER-SHIRRING

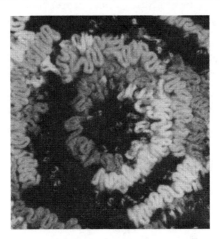

Basic sewn center shirring is one of my favorite ways to make a rug. It is a very simple process but the results can be simply fabulous. The landscape rug on the cover is a sewn center shirred rug. The design possibilities for this type of rug are endless and they really can be a fine example of folk art when they are done.

Basic center shirring is a two-step process that can be done with fabric strips of a wide variety of widths. First, the fabric strips are gathered with needle and thread. The shirred strips are then sewn together to make the rug.

You can use any long embroidery needle, though the easiest to work with is a long (4 to 5-inch) embroidery or soft sculpture needle. Blunt-tipped needles work well and save your fingers. The gathering thread can be mercerized crochet thread, heavy upholstery thread or 3-ply unwaxed linen.

In sewn center shirring the fabric strips are gathered with a simple running stitch, made by working the needle in and out of the fabric with about a half inch between stitches. It requires only a little practice to make even, straight stitches in strips of fabric.

The process of sewn center shirring is so simple, and the rugs so easy to make, that for some time I had been mystified as to why the Shakers didn't make them. Instead, they gathered long strips of fabric and stitched them to a base fabric. These "caterpillar" rugs took just as long to make as a shirred rug, so why not? The answer I think is in the "caterpillars" themselves. In the process of getting organized for this new edition, I found some sewn center shirred sections that I had made twenty years ago and never used. They were made before I learned that shirred fabric should not be packed tightly on the gathering threads. The folds of fabric were thoroughly twisted around the thread and straightening out one section only led to worse twisting in the next. No wonder I hadn't used them—in my early shirring days, I was making "caterpillars," just like the Shakers.

Above is a collection of my old caterpillars. Notice how round they are with all of the folds twisted around the thread.

This is what a center shirred strip should look like. The folds are snug together, but not so tightly packed that the section won't lay straight.

The easiest way to keep from creating caterpillars is to squeeze the gathered strip, from the knot toward the needle. If the folds shift toward the needle, they are packed too tightly. Of course, you don't want the folds to be so far apart that the gathering thread shows either. With some practice, you'll develop an eye for the right spacing.

In the illustrations that follow, heavy wool is shown since it photographs more clearly than thinner wool. Using heavy wool in sewn center shirring is perfectly fine, and the work goes more quickly. However, for the characteristically velvet texture, lighter wools are best. To combine the best of both worlds, shir two strips of light wool at the same time.

As always, I recommend that your first project be a small one so that you can perfect your technique before proceeding to make a rug. The sewn center shirred chairpad is ideal for this. It is small enough to allow you to complete it quickly. And by the time you're finished, you'll have mastered the basics of shirring so that you can tackle larger projects with confidence.

SEWN CENTER SHIRRED CHAIRPAD

This center shirred chairpad will measure 16-18 inches in diameter depending on the weight of the wool that you use. Heavier wool will make up larger. Fleece or old sweaters are also good choices. See the Handbook section for tips on how to cut various fabrics or recycle clothing for these rugs.

Materials: About 4 yards (45" wide) of skirt weight wool or wool blend fabric. (This is roughly equivalent to two old skirts.) Thread: One ball of mercerized cotton crochet thread of a neutral color.
Cut the fabric into strips 3/4 to 1 inch wide, on the bias of the fabric.

SHIRRING THE STRIPS

1. Thread the needle with 5 or 6 feet of thread. The thread is used doubled. Knot the ends together. The distance between the needle and the knot should not be longer than three feet.

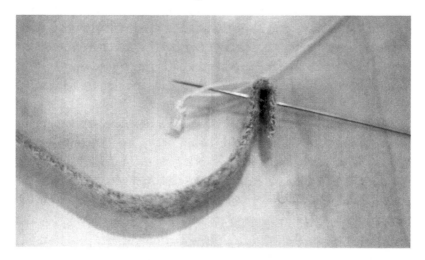

2. Insert the needle into the center of the first strip, about 1/4 inch from the end, then pass the needle back through the thread loop. This is done to securely anchor the knot. Pull up the thread.

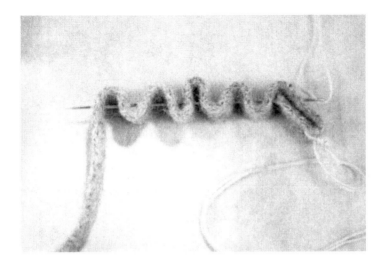

3. Using a running stitch in the center of the strip, sew the entire length of the strip. Place the stitches as evenly as possible, about a half inch apart. When the strip is entirely stitched, push it down the thread until it is held by the knotted end. Then stitch the next strip just the same way, and push it down the thread.

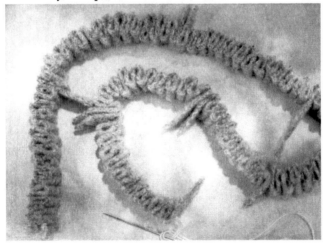

4. When the thread is nearly filled with shirred strips, it is time to knot off the thread and begin a new thread. Note that the shirred strips should be packed snugly along the thread, but do not force the folds so tightly that the shirring is forced to twist around the thread.

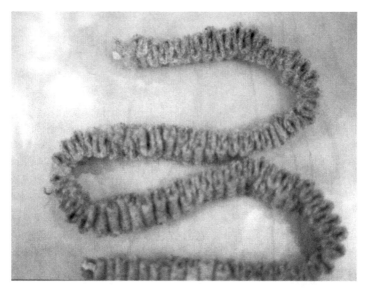

5. Adjust the shirred strips so that they are "squeezably soft" and knot the thread at that point. There will be ends of the strip that stick up above the folds. Clip these off so that they are even. Don't worry if the shirred pieces aren't aligned perfectly at this point. They will be straightened out as the rug is stitched together.

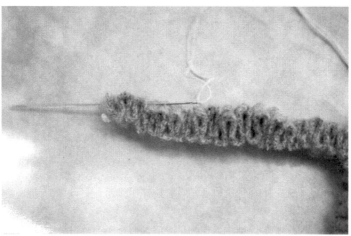

Decide if you want to work with a continuous length of shirring or separate smaller sections. To make a continuous length, thread the needle, double the thread and knot the end. Insert the needle into the shirred strip a couple of folds ahead of where the previous thread was knotted. Then continue shirring as before.

If you are planning to work a design with blocks of color, the shirred strips should be left as individual units.

STITCHING IT TOGETHER

For a chairpad, you will need 25 to 30 feet of shirred fabric (depending on the weight of the fabric). You will want to begin coiling and assembly when the shirring reaches about 6 feet long. (If you made the shirred pieces separately, coiling can begin as soon as the first section is ready.)

To begin assembly, make sure that all of the folds along the thread are straight. Since shirring tends to twist around the thread, simply rotate the folds so that they all face the same way. Thread a needle with five to six feet of thread, double the thread and knot the ends.

Working on a flat surface, coil the center of the chairpad so that it has two or three complete rounds of shirring around it.

Work on a flat surface and make sure that your coil of shirring has the top and botton edges lined up and it is round in shape. The coil of shirring should be firm, but don't pull on the shirred section to make it extra tight.

As you stitch the center, make sure that the thread is pulled snugly, but don't stitch so tightly that it distorts the round shape.

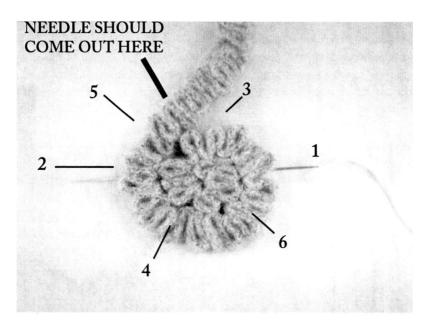

NEEDLE SHOULD
COME OUT HERE

5

3

2

1

6

4

Stitch completely through the coil (from #1 to #2 in the illustration below). Pull the thread up snugly.

Rotate the coil slightly and stitch back through the center (from #2 to #3)

Rotate and stitch again following the illustration so that there are at least six stitches all of the way through the center coil. Take extra stitches if you need to so that the needle comes out at the outer edge of the shirred strip as shown in the photo.

Pull the thread snug between each stitch, but don't pull the thread so tightly that the round shape gets flattened. If you do a lot of handsewing, you will likely be pulling too hard on the thread. Pull only until you feel a little resistance from the wool.

When you are finished, the center should be firm and generally round. If it feels loose, add a few more stitches. If it looks lop-sided, the stitching has been pulled too tightly. After the center stitching, the assembly is continued by using a fairly large back-stitch.

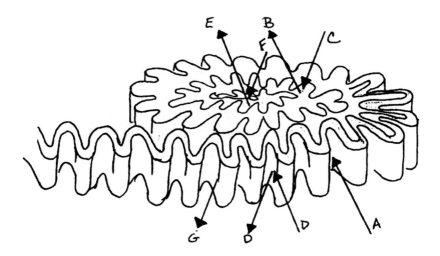

Work in the same direction as the coil. Insert the needle at "A", between the folds, and bring it out at "B". For the next stitch, insert the needle at "C" (where the thread emerges) and bring it out at "D" (about 2 to 3 folds away).

Then stitch in angling upwards at "D" again, coming out at "E". Stitch down at "F" (where the thread emerges) coming out at "G". This stitching pattern is continued through the body of the rug or chairpad.

Practice inserting and ending each stitch between folds at the outside edge. In the center of the rug, the stitch should always be started exactly where the thread comes out from the previous stitch. Make sure that all of the stitches penetrate at least one previous round of shirring.

Center shirred projects should always be assembled on a flat surface. If you have a lap board you can use it for small projects like the chair pad. Larger rugs will need to be assembled on a table.

The Final Stitches

When you reach the end of the last shirred section, make at least two stitches securing the final fold. Pull the fold to the edge of the chairpad or rug to hide the knot. Insert the needle into the shirring toward the center of the rug, bringing it up between any two folds. Knot the thread so that the knot slips down into the rug and is hidden. Clip off the thread and you're done.

If your chairpad does not lay perfectly flat, you can steam it with a damp tea towel under a hot iron. Then let the pad dry flat. As a general rule, if the pad has a tendency to cup, you have coiled the shirring too tightly or made your stitches too tightly; if it waves at the edges, you have packed the shirring too closely around the edge. If you notice either cupping or waving consistently, use safetypins to secure each round before stitching it to the rug. The pins help to keep the shirred strip properly placed.

If you make sure to assemble the project on a flat surface, most problems can be avoided. Center shirring is a forgiving technique, and even major errors in assembly will cure themselves with time and use.

The most important thing when beginning an oval rug, is to make sure that the center section is p e r f e c t l y straight.

If it curves or bulges, remove the stitching and redo it. For long oval centers, I suggest basting the sections together to make sure that they stay lined up. Any curve in the center will continue in the rug for several rows, so make sure that it is begun in a straight line.

Another option for beginning a rug is to use many different small centers. They can be lined upin a row, and then surrounded by rounds of shirring.

Small round centers arranged in a triangle or diamondcan be used to create a unique shape.

Small rounds centers can also be assembled in offset rows, and then bordered, or you can also make an entire rug of small round centers, just like the *milleflore* beaded rugs discusssed previously.

When planning a new rug, the first inclination is to dream of a room size rug, which is generally not the best choice. A room size shirred rug may require years to complete and most often large dream rugs are abandoned long before they reach room size. Very large shirred rugs also present difficulties in cleaning, turning and care.

Fortunately a shirred rug can be finished off at any point so that if you find you have run out of energy for rug making, none of your effort will be wasted, you will simply have a smaller rug. When ending an oval rug, make sure that the shirring strip ends along one of the curved ends (not along one of the straight sides). That will disguise the end of the shirred strip.

Center shirred rugs should generally be 1/2 to 1 inch thick. If you are making a rug that is going to be walked on, keep the width to 3/4-inch or less.   (If you make a one inch thick rug, you will need to taper the edges to minimize tripping hazards. See the Handbook section for a discussion of edge sculpting.)

Shading from One Color to Another
When you have a lot of different colors of fabrics to use in the same rug, you can create a striped rug or a hit-or-miss pattern like the rug shown in progress at the beginning of this section. Those aren't the only choices, and sometimes the contrasts in the fabrics are too stark for a well-designed rug. If you have that type of material, you can create a more sophisticated rug by blending the colors as you shir them.

The shirring is done with two strips at a time. If the fabrics are closely related in tone or color, the blending will be very subtle in the rug. Use that technique to provide transitions from one color to another.

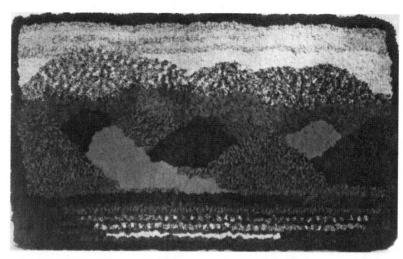

PIECED DESIGNS WITH LONG STRIPS

The most interesting (and fun) center shirred rugs are those that are made by what is called the "piecing" method. This allows blocks of color and lines to be used to form an elaborate design and/or a custom shape.

The landscape rug on the cover is a sewn center-shirred rug constructed by this piecing method. The photo below shows the same rug as it was being made, with fairly short shirred sections of a single fabric.

For a pictoral design, begin with a sketch outlining the major elements of your design. Don't try to get too detailed. You will need to include a solid foreground and background or several solid border rows to make sure that the rug will be strong enough for long years of handling. (The landscape rug includes both.)

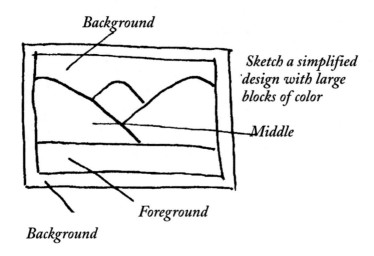

Background

Sketch a simplified design with large blocks of color

Middle

Foreground

Background

For this example, the foreground is assembled first as long solid lines, stitched together, back and forth across the width of the rug.

When the foreground is complete, begin stitching the first element of the middle ground.

Once the foreground is stitched, the first element of the middle of the design is added, working back and forth attaching it to the foreground. Each element of the design is stitched the same way. Always work the major elements of the design where they have the most contact with other elements.

Steps to completing a design with long shirred strips

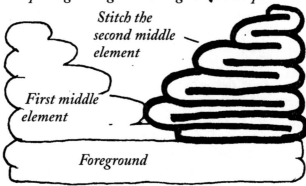

Stitch the
second middle
element

First middle
element

Foreground

Fill in the middle elements

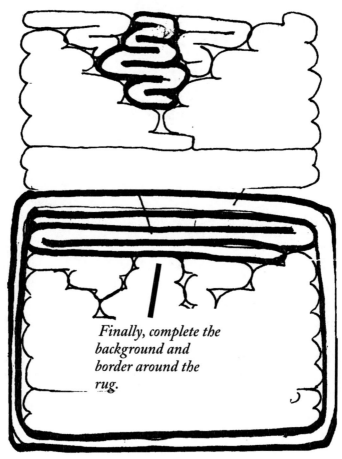

Finally, complete the
background and
border around the
rug.

Small design features are worked to fill in between the major elements. Though the sketches show these features worked horizontally back and forth, it is often convenient to stitch the shirring at an angle along the face of a major design feature.

These rugs can be abstract or pictorial. You can use this method to create a center shirred rug in any shape.

Pieced rugs, no matter how complex the designs, really should have a border of uninterrupted shirring. A minimum of two rounds of border shirring will help the rug to maintain its shape and give it strength.

PIECED DESIGNS WITH SHORT SHIRRED SECTIONS

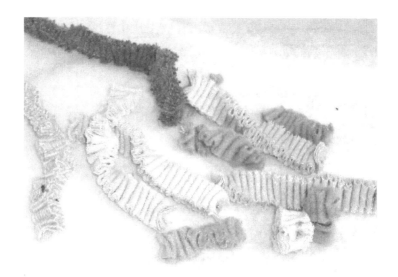

For adding details to a rug, or for a rug with a very elaborate design, you can use very short sections of sewn center shirring. These small sections are sewn individually to the rug to gradually build up a design.

In the following example, short sections of shirring are pieced to develop a floral motif, about a foot in diameter. The motif could be repeated all over a rug, or could be used as the center of a rug.

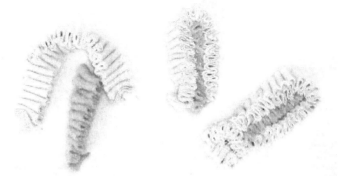

To begin the flower, make one small round piece, five petal centers about 2.5 inches long and five outer petals about 6 inches long, shirred separately. Above left, are the sections for one petal. In the center, those two have been sewn together and at the right, the petal is shown stitched to the round center.

Each of the five petals is stitched to the center, forming a five-pointed star shape. You can use fewer petals with the small center, but if you want to create a design with more petals, the center circle will need to be made larger.

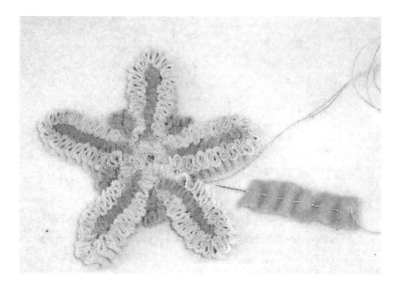

To fill the "V" formed by two petals, a very short (one inch) section of shirring is added. Because the shirring is so short (just six folds), it is shirred onto the needle and then sewn directly to the floral center.

Below, a border row has been added, and again small shirred sections are sewn into the "V" between the petals.

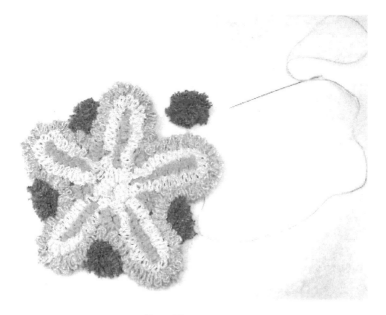

Another border row is added (above) and then outer petals are begun. For these, short lengths of shirring are built up in the lowest part of the flower, to form a generally rounder shape.

Finally, the outer petals are edged with a contrasting color to complete the motif as shown on this page.

This technique of using very short strips of sewn center shirring can be expanded to an entire rug. There is unlimited design potential and it lends itself to the use of small, leftover scraps of fabric.

CHAPTER 8

AN INTRODUCTION TO CROCHETED SHIRRING

Crocheted center shirring is the most popular of the shirred rugs (which, admittedly isn't saying much since it isn't really all that well known). The crocheted techniques make reliably soft and spongy shirred rugs, and anyone familiar with crocheting can learn to adapt it to rug making.

One advantage that crocheted shirring has over the sewn techniques of shirring is that the crochet stitches automatically space the folds yielding a softer texture in the finished project. That makes these techniques adapatable to cotton fabrics, especially denim. By contrast, cotton sewn center-shirred rugs can have a surface that is too hard, especially if the folds are packed tightly. Crocheting prevents this from happening.

There are three basic types of crocheted shirring, representing the steps in the development of the process. Once someone discovered that folds of fabric could be shirred onto a crochet hook and then crocheted off to make a long strip, the next question was how to join the strips to create a rug. Most simply, the strips could be stitched together just like sewn center shirring. Second, the strips could be crocheted together to form a rug and finally, the strips could be crocheted together as they were formed so the rug construction was completed in a single step.

The two earliest methods are the simplest, but because they did not require a special tool, they didn't lend themselves to mass marketing efforts. Examples of both are pretty much confined to pre-WW1. The more complex third method did survive thanks largely to the marketing of specially bent, notched or "hump backed" afghan hooks. Even this method was a novelty by the 1950s.

The first technique (**crochet, then sew**) I am calling the **"Snow-on-the-Mountain"** technique named after a turn of the century rug which used it. The rug was made of a houndstooth wool, which created a speckled rug surface, fancifully resembling a snow covered mountain. The method can, of course, be used with any suitable fabric. This type of crocheted shirring can be handled and used for any of the same assembly methods described for sewn center-shirring, including pieced designs and freeform rugs. It is significantly softer than standing wool techniques, so it shouldn't be used in combination with them for a rug, but such a combination would be fine in wall hangings or art pieces.

The intermediate technique (**crocheted in two steps**) I am calling the **"two-hook"** method since it is most easily done with an afghan hook for the shirring step and a steel crochet hook for the assembly. Both steps can be done with the same hook, so two hooks really aren't required, just recommended for ease of handling.

The third and most complicated technique (**shirred and crocheted in a single step**) I refer to as the **"bent hook"** method since specially modified afghan hooks are so closely associated with it. It should be noted that the method can be done with a plain afghan hook or even a small standard crochet hook.

If you are new to crocheted shirring, I would suggest that you tackle these methods in order—even if you just make a small sample of each to try them out. The simplest method is also the fastest, and the most complex is the slowest. Since it takes an expert's examination to tell the finished rugs apart, so you may find that you are perfectly happy with the simpler technique. (Note: In previous editions, I'd included the crocheted faux shirring alongside the other crocheted center shirring methods. For clarification in this edition, that method is now presented in Chapter 5 associated with other faux shirring methods.)

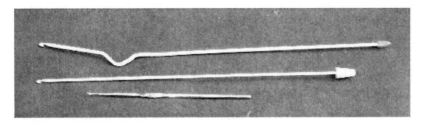

HOOKS FOR CROCHETED SHIRRING

For any of the crocheted shirring methods, you will need an afghan hook, in a size from 1.5mm or 2.5mm or a steel crochet hook size 5 to 8. The point of the hook should be small enough to penetrate the fabric easily yet still large enough to control the thread. (If you have a "bent" hook it will work fine with any of these methods instead of an afghan hook.)

The advantage of an afghan hook is that it lets you shir a lot of strips at a single time. A steel crochet hook works just fine to make these rugs, but you can only shir a small section of folds at a time. If you are working a pattern for which you need to count folds, using the small hook is actually a better choice.

Afghan hooks are available in steel or aluminum. The steel hooks will last longer but are more expensive and can be difficult to find. Afghan hooks that work best with crocheted shirring have a hook at one end and a pointed tip at the other. Often the pointed tip is covered by a twist off cap or a rubber stopper, for safety and to keep the fabric folds from sliding off the back end of the hook. (If your hook doesn't have a back stopper, use a pencil eraser to make your own.)

The pointed end has a second purpose. If you are shirring with heavy wool, denim or other densely woven fabric, you can use the pointed end of the hook as a needle to do the shirring. Often, with these sorts of fabric, it is a struggle to shir from the hook end, so the point does come in handy. If the pointed end of your afghan hook develops a burr or gets dull, you can resharpen it with a steel file or (for aluminum hooks) an emery board.

Threads and Fabrics for Crocheted Shirring

As for all of the shirred and standing wool rugs, the strength of the rug depends on the quality of the thread which is used to hold it together. Good quality mercerized crochet cotton or 3-ply linen are good choices.

Almost any resilient fabric can be used to make a crocheted shirring rug. The rug will increase in size most quickly with heavier fabrics, but will have a more velvety surface with lighter and more open weaves. Experiment with a variety of fabrics.

Cut woven fabrics into strips on the bias, usually ¾-inch wide, and don't worry about squaring off the ends. That is done after the folds have been shirred onto the hook. Felted fabrics can be cut in any direction and knits should be cut in the direction of the least stretch. For how to prepare other fabrics and recycle clothing for these rugs, see the Handbook section.

CHAPTER 9

SNOW-ON-THE-MOUNTAIN CROCHETED SHIRRING

This type of crocheted shirring is by far the easiest. It is done in two steps, using a small diameter afghan hook is used to do the shirring, and then the shirred chain is sewn together, just as for sewn center-shirred rugs.

Shirring the Fabric onto the Hook

Clip the end of the fabric strip off so that it has a square end. Insert the afghan hook into the fabric strip, about ¼ inch from the end. Work the hook in and out of the strip at about ½-inch intervals. Don't

include any tapered ends in the shirring. When one strip is shirred in this way, start the next strip and continue shirring fabric onto the hook until the hook is almost full. Match the ends of each of the strips so that they both point the same way. When the hook is full, clip off any strip ends that stick out past the folds.

Make a slip knot in the crochet thread, place it on the end of the hook.

Draw the loop of thread through one complete fold of the fabric, working the fabric off of the hook at the same time. You will need to lift the fold slightly to work it over the hook.

Then pull another loop of thread through the thread loop on the hook (chain 1). Pull another loop of thread through the loop on the hook (chain a second time).

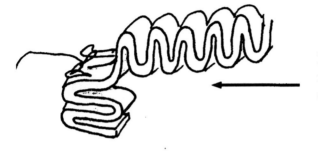

Pull off another fold and then chain 2.

Repeat alternately pulling off a fold and chaining two stitches until all of the fabric folds have been worked off of the hook. That's all there is to it!

When you come to the end of a shirred piece of fabric, it may end with a complete fold, so you just begin the next strip also with a complete fold. If you have a fabric strip that just has an end flap (not a fold) pull it off as well as the end flap of the next strip. Two strip ends count as one fold, which is why the ends get lined up as you shir the fabric onto the hook.

When all of the fabric strip has been crocheted off the hook, pull up the thread loop. This is just to keep it from slipping back through the completed stitches and acts as a little bit of safety while you use the hook to shir on more fabric strips. Fill the hook with more shirred strips, clip the ends even and repeat the process of crocheting them off. This makes a long continuous shirred "chain" of folds ready to assemble into a rug.

Examine the chain of shirring folds. The thread loops show on one side and the other shows only the folds. (If you spread the folds, you can see the chain stitch inside.)

It is not necessary that the rug be composed of a single, long uninterrupted chain. If you want to work with shorter chained sections that is fine. To end a chain of crocheted shirring, complete the two chain stitches after any fold. Clip the thread and pull the end of the thread up through the last chain stitch.

Assembling the Rug

For a Snow-on-the-Mountain rug, the crocheted chains are sewn together just as the sewn center shirring rugs in Chapter 7, so refer to the directions there.

Crocheted chains can be used most easily for round, oval and striped rugs. Notice that the crocheted chains have a little give and will stretch if they are forced to. As you stitch a crocheted chain to the rug, be sure not to pull on the chain or the rug will begin to cup. The easiest way to prevent cupping is to place the crocheted chain next to the rug and safety pin it every few inches.

Crocheted chains also make a good edge finish for crocheted faux shirring. Because the thread only shows on one side, the chain will give a faux shirred rug a border with only folds showing on the outside.

Then make a single crochet stitch in the very first "fold space" of the shirred chain.

Make a single crochet in the next stitch on the wrong side, then another into the very first fold space (same place as last time).

Around the first row, there will be one single crochet stitch for each chain stitch on the wrong side of the chain. In order to make the rug lay flat, two stitches are placed in the same fold space around the center.

Complete the <u>first round</u> of single crochet stitches working one stitch in each chain stitch on the "wrong" side of the shirred chain and then one into a fold space. There should be two single crochet stitches in each fold space around until you reach the safety pin. (The pin marks the end of the first row of crocheting.)

The rug is continued in the same way. One single crochet is always placed in each space on the "wrong" side of the chain and then a single crochet is made in a fold space.

For the **second round** of crocheting, there are two stitches made in every second fold space.

For the third round, two stitches are made in every third fold space. In the fourth round, every fourth fold space and so on. As the rug gets larger, it is easier to mark the position of the doubled-up stitches with small safety pins instead of counting stitches.

The above increase pattern will work on almost every fabric, but if you begin to notice the rug begin to cup, make **one round** with 12 evenly spaced doubled stitches in it. Then resume using six double-up stitches in the next round.

If you rug begins to full-up, or form a wave, make **one row** with NO doubled-up stitches, then resume with six in each row.

When the rug is nearly of the size you want, make the final round without any doubled-up stitches. To finish off, just bring the end of the crochet thread up through the last loop on the hook to end off, and clip the thread at least six inches away from the knot. Use a sewing needle to work the end of the crochet thread back into the rug.

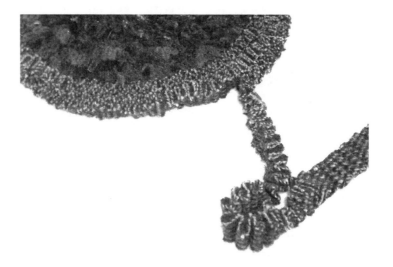

OVAL RUGS

Fold the shirred chain in half so that the "wrong" sides of the chain line up. The folded section will be the difference between the finished length and width of the rug.

For example, if you want a rug that is five feet long and three feet wide, the center folded section should be two feet long. (5 - 3 = 2). The stitches showing on the folded section should line up with each other, with one space at the end.

Place a slip knot on the end of the steel crochet hook, and slide the hook under both threads of both chain stitches next to the fold. Complete a single crochet stitch which will attach the two sides together. Chain 1.

Then insert the hook under the threads of the next matching pair, and single crochet again and chain 1. This continues until you reach the end of the folded section.

From this point on, a single crochet stitch will be made alternately under a chain stitch on the "wrong" side of the shirred chain, and then into the fold space at the center of the rug. (No additional chain stitches are used between the single crochet stitches.) This alternate side-to-side stitching proceed along the side of the oval.

In order to make the rug lay flat, doubled-up stitches are used in three fold spaces around the ends of the rug. Mark the position of these doubled stitches with safety pins at each end of the rug.

In the first round of stitching at the end of the rug, three fold spaces in a row will have two single crochet stitches. In the second round, every other fold space will have doubled-up stitches. In the third round, every third fold space; fourth round every fourth fold space, and so on. As the rug gets larger, it is easier to use three small safety pins to mark the location of 3 doubled-up stitches at each end rather than counting stitches.

There are no doubled-up stitches along the sides of the oval. Each side is continued with a single crochet stitch placed alternately on the wrong side of the outer shirring and in the fold space of the rug center.

If the rug begins to cup or to wave adjust the number of doubled up stitches at the ends just like for a round rug above.

SQUARE AND RECTANGULAR RUGS

To start a square, follow the round directions through two complete rounds. To start a rectangle, follow the oval directions through two complete rounds.

Using small safety pins, mark four evenly spaced corners. In the fold-space at each of the corners, place three single crochets. (Only one single crochet is placed in all of the other fold-spaces.) That's all there is to it.

HEART-SHAPED RUGS

The two-hook technique is really the only shirring method that will form a reliably regular heart-shaped rug. To create a heart, think of it as an oval rug with a bend in the middle of it. The lobes of the heart are formed exactly like the ends of an oval rug. The point of the heart is the same as a square corner. The notch (opposite the point) is formed by skipping a fold space entirely.

STRIPED RUGS

The shirred chain is folded back and forth in a continuous S-curve to form a striped rug. Although the rug can be a single color, or many colors of fabric, the assembly pattern will give the rug a striped appearance. The shirred chain can be folded to form stripes, which run either the width or the length of the rug.

Fold the shirred chain in half so that the "wrong" sides of the chain line up. The folded section will be either the finished length or the width of the rug.

Place a slip knot on the end of the steel crochet hook, and slide the hook under both threads of both chain stitches next to the fold. Complete a single crochet stitch, which will attach the two sides together. Chain 1.

Then insert the hook under the threads of the next matching pair, and single crochet again and chain 1. This continues until you reach the end of the folded section. Now you are ready to turn it over and work back in the opposite direction.

With the crochet hook, chain two stitches. Then remove the thread from the hook. Take the hook to the top of the work and push it through the end fold. Hook the thread and pull it through. Now you can begin working the next row. This row will have two "right" sides facing, so the single crochet stitches will be done in the fold spaces. Leave the very first fold space unstitched.

Complete the row by making a single crochet in each fold space, then one chain stitch. Repeat the sequence with the matching fold space.

When you reach the end of the row, turn the work over and fold the shirred chain back the other direction. Chain up just like you did at the end of the first row, and pull the thread through the first fold on the next row. This time the "wrong" sides of the shirred chain line up so it is done just like the very first row.

Continue with crocheting the rows together until the rug is the size you want. Cover the end threads with a small crocheted chain.

CHAPTER 11

CROCHETED SHIRRING: BENT HOOK METHOD

The "bent hook" method of crocheted shirring creates rugs in a single step. Because you will be working crochet stitches while the fabric strip is on the hook, you must be able to positively control the tip of the hook to keep it from rotating in your hand.

In the twentieth century, bent hooks began as simple reverse-curved afghan hooks (the hook points away from the bend). The bend made the hook less likely to turn in the hand. If you've ever run across a long

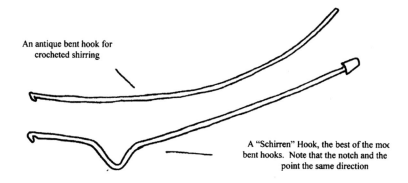

An antique bent hook for
crocheted shirring

A "Schirren" Hook, the best of the moc
bent hooks. Note that the notch and the
point the same direction

crochet hook in an antique store with that shape, that bend wasn't accidental. Some old bent hooks had a triangular cross-section in the center of the shaft, which kept the hook bent and also improved the rug maker's grip.

Following World War I, afghan hooks with a notch ("hump-backed hooks") began to appear. Marketed under several trade names, all of these hooks had the notch pointing the same direction as the hook and were controlled by placing the middle finger in the notch. Most of the early companies marketing these hooks were out of business by the 1960s, but the "Rugbee" hook and "Shirret"(TM) hook replaced them. A special mention should be made of the late Sophie Wold of the Seattle area who developed elaborately patterned (counted folds) designs and taught numerous students her techniques. Her influence can be quickly spotted in vintage bent-hook rugs, and inspired other manufacturers to offer more complex designs for the rugs.

In the 1960s, Louise McCrady coined the term "shirret" ™ by combining "shirring" and "crochet" and began marketing a bent hook. Her pattern innovation was to include chaining up between rounds of crocheted shirring, rather than the older spiral method. The "Rugbee" hook and "crinkle crochet" were competitor's trade names for crocheted shirring. Because none of the various instructions during the era included a reliable pattern for increasing, there were quite a few small rugs made, but larger rugs were fairly rare.

In the 1990s, LACIS of Berkeley redesigned the hook with the notch pointing in the same direction as the hook. Their "schirren" hook could be controlled with the thumb, which was a more natural grip for most crocheters. In addition, the handle incorporated a slight bend, in the style of the original bent hooks.

BASICS

You do not need a specially bent hook to use this method. A straight afghan hook can be used if you do not overload it with folds. A standard steel crochet hook can also be used. You just can't shir quite as many folds of fabric onto it at one time. Actually, I prefer using a standard steel hook when working a pattern with counted folds. The folds are shirred onto the hook one fabric at a time and it makes the process a little more straightforward. You can also bend an afghan hook yourself or purchase a notched afghan hook.

Fabric strip is shirred onto a bent afghan hook in exactly the same manner as for the Snow-on-the-Mountain technique and the two hook method in the preceding chapters.

The most common bent hook rugs are created by alternating "straight" and "increase" rounds in the round and oval shapes, which can be confusing for beginners, so I've found it easier to teach an older style first.

Bent Hook Shirring for the Beginner

This type of crocheted shirring has come into and out of fashion several times with the introduction of various brands of commercially marketed bent hooks. One of the reasons it remains relatively unknown is that the directions that were (and still are) sent with the hooks were sketchy and generally confusing.

Originally, I'd been quite puzzled that this method evolved at all since it did not appear to be a logical extension of any of the other methods. It was not until I was teaching a class several years ago and trying to help a student who just couldn't grasp the method that I said to her, "Think of it like filet crochet." Then the light dawned. This method wasn't just "like" filet crochet, it *was* filet crochet—and the folds of fabric substituted for the chain stitches. Someone had experimented and found that shirring and filet crochet could be combined. In the late 19th and early 20th centuries, filet crochet was a widely used technique so the timing of the development of the rugs was also understandable. I was fairly certain that in the early stages, people used regular steel crochet hooks for the rugs, rather than the specialized afghan hooks, which were marketed after WWI, and I came to prefer the steel crochet hooks myself.

From that point forward, I had a simplified method for teaching bent hook rugs, and did away with the afghan hooks entirely for beginners, since the regular hooks were so much easier for students to manage. In essence, I found that if I taught people in the same sequence that the technique developed, it was much easier to learn. Beginning with filet crochet idea, also allowed me to teach beginners how to create patterns in their very first practice piece. So, if you have tried commercial directions and given up on these rugs, try just one more time with this approach.

Beginners Project
To get started, don't worry about buying any special supplies. You'll need a standard steel crochet hook (size 5 to 8), some cotton crochet thread and ¾-inch bias-cut fabric strips in two or three different colors.

In the example shown, the strips are of a skirt weight wool, but feel free to use any fabrics you have on hand. As long as the crochet hook will go through the fabric, it will do fine for the practice piece. For how to prepare other fabrics, follow the instructions in the Handbook section.) Since this is for practice, don't worry about perfection.

Directions:

Attach the thread to the hook with a slip knot and chain 22.

Page 113

Take the yarn off of the hook.

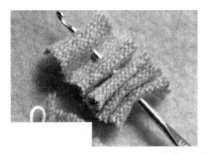

Have then ends of your fabric strip squared off, and work the fabric strip over the end of the crochet hook, back and forth about ½ inch apart, to make five complete folds of fabric on the hook. Put the last chain stitch back onto the hook.

Gently pull one fold of fabric off the hook, while keeping the chain stitch on the hook. You'll be pulling the chain stitch through the fold of fabric, so try not to catch any of the fabric threads with the hook.

Make one d o u b l e crochet stitch in the second chain from the hook.

Pull the second fold of fabric off the hook, pulling the crochet thread through it. Then skip one chain stitch and make a double crochet.
Pull off the third fold, skip one chain and double crochet.
Pull of the fourth fold, skip one chain and double crochet.
Pull off the fifth fold, skip one chain and double crochet.

Remove the crochet hook from the thread loop, and shir five more folds onto the hook.

Pull of the next fold, skip one chain stitch and double crochet.
Repeat for each fold on the hook. The final double crochet after the last fold should go into the original chain stitch, but if it doesn't, don't worry about it. The practice piece is designed for just the ten folds of fabric, so that it goes quickly.

To begin the next row, chain 3, then remove the hook from the thread loop and shir more folds onto the hook. If you can easily handle the hook with more than five folds, that's great, just don't overfill

the hook so that it gets awkward to handle.

Put the last chain stitch back on the hook. Then pull off one fold.

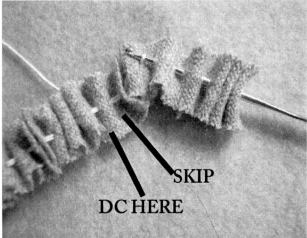

SKIP

DC HERE

2 STRIP ENDS
COUNT AS 1 FOLD

Skip the first space, and insert a double crochet in the space between the next two folds. Work under both threads that are visible.

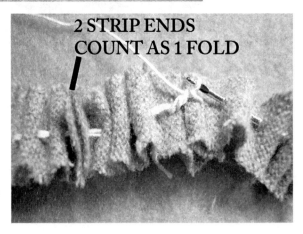

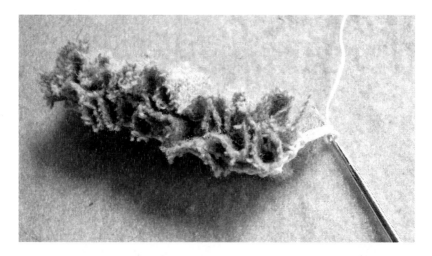

Pull off the next fold. Double crochet in the space between the next two folds. Repeat this process across the row. (Two strip ends count as one fold, so don't place a double crochet stitch between the two ends. See the photo on the previous page.)

If you run out of folds on the hook, simply stop **after a double crochet** stitch and shir more folds onto the hook. When you have completed removing the folds, finish the row with a double crochet into the double crochet stitch visible at the outer edge of the folds. The photo above shows the second row of folds completed.

To begin the third row (and all rows from here on), chain 3.
Remove the thread loop from the hook and shir on more folds of fabric.
Put the last chain stitch back on the hook.
Skip the first space and double crochet in the space between the next two folds.
Pull off a loop of fabric, double crochet in the next space and repeat to the end of the row.
Finish the row with a double crochet stitch into the double crochet at the outside edge.

Stop as necessary to shir more folds of fabric onto the hook.

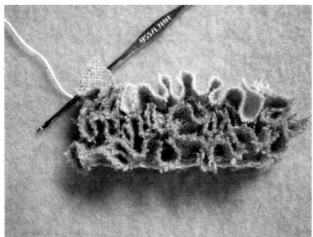

It's your choice if you want to continue with the sample using only one color until you are comfortable with the procedure, but I've found that it is more exciting for beginners to be able to see a pattern develop in about third row. So, for this type of sample with a total of 10 folds, the third row is begun with only **two folds** of Color 1 shirred onto the hook. Crochet them off, then shir on **six folds** of Color 2. Crochet them off. Shir on **two folds** of Color 1 and crochet them off and end the row with a double crochet. The finished row is shown above.

The fourth and fifth row have Color 1--2 folds; Color 2--2 folds; Color 3--2 folds; Color 2--2 folds; Color 1--2 folds. (At this point don't try to shir with more than one color on the hook at a time.)

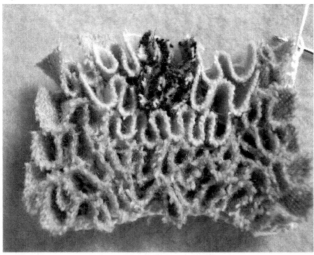

The sixth row is the same as the third row. The seventh and eighth row are solid using only Color 1 just like the first two rows. End the sample after the last double crochet in a any row, by making a chain stitch and pulling up the end of the clipped thread.

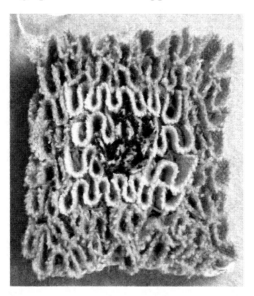

Most of my students immediately want to try another sample piece with a design of their own, or a differeant fabric. What I find most gratifying is that the first sample is usually completed in about an hour, and the students have a good understanding of how patterns are created as well, desmystifying the whole process.

This method isn't just for samples, though. It is expandable to rugs of any size. For example, to add to the sample piece, along the chain stitched edge, you would work in every other chain stitch, just as you did for the first row. To add along the sides where the double crochet stitches show, work two fold+double crochet in each of the double crochet stitches. To add to the top, just continue with the regular process of a fold plus a double crochet. These strategies also form a nice border, so the crochet thread doesn't show at the outer edge of the rug.

For very large rugs, you can make several sections of shirring and then piece them together. If you're aiming for a large rug, this is a good tactic to adopt because large rugs can get quite heavy to handle.

For example, you can make a central section that is two feet wide and three feet long and then make narrower sections for borders that are added one at a time, using the 2-hook method in the previous chapter to crochet them together. Of course, these border strips have to be made to the exact measurement of the central section. Your rug can continue to grow by adding as many sections as you like.

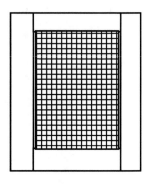

Patterns for Shirred Rugs on a Grid
Because this technique has straight lines and rows, you create your own designs by sketching them on graph paper. If you aren't confident of your own design talents, you can use any charted pattern as a basis for a rug. Patterns for cross-stitch or filet crochet work fine, but don't overlook the patterns for traditional hooked rugs and even latch hook rugs which are also presented in grids. Basically, you can recreate almost any design if you can make a grid over it.

Start with fairly simple motifs like squares, crosses or diamonds before you attempt elaborate floral patterns, since accurately counting out the folds back and forth in charted rows does take a little practice.

Graduating to an Afghan Hook
The advantage of using an afghan hook in this type of crocheted shirring is simply that you can shir more folds at a time, which does make the process a little faster. However, afghan hooks and the specially bent hooks can just be too awkward to handle, so if you're having trouble, just stay with the steel crochet hook.

The trickiest part for beginners is learning to shir on the counted folds in the right order. With an afghan hook, remove the back cap and always shir the folds on from that end. Shir the colors in the order

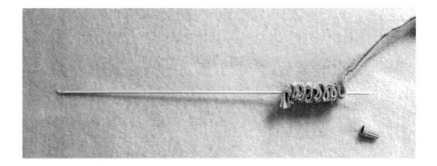

they will be crocheted and they will be in the proper sequence on the afghan hook.

Using an afghan hook also makes it easier to begin this type of shirring with a shirred chain. The folds are shirred onto the hook and crocheted off with chain stitches, so you can begin the design from the very first stitches. See the Snow-on-the-Mountain rug for detailed instructions for making base chains.

Working Round and Oval Rugs
If you want to create rugs other than squares or rectangles the bent-hook method can worked around and around for round and oval rugs. Because the basic stitch is the same as the grid-style rugs, the approach has to be modifed around curves to allow for the increasing diameter of the rugs.

In most kinds of crocheted rugs, "increases" are made by using two stitches. With this type of construction, however, increases are made by regularly pulling off two folds, rather than making additional stitches. Of course, in the following row, there will be a stitch between both of the folds so the end result is the same. It just doesn't show like doubled-up crochet stitches would.

In the following directions, a bent-hook is illustrated, but you can use an afghan hook (1.5mm to 2.5mm) or a standard steel crochet (size 5 to 8).

CROCHETING A ROUND RUG

Have the hook fully loaded with fabric strip, with all ends trimmed evenly. Use a good quality, mercerized crochet thread, and make a slip knot on the hook.

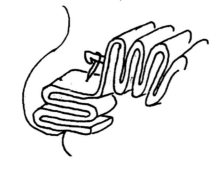

Gently slip two complete folds off the end of the hook, pulling the slip knot through the folds.

With the thread, chain 2. Gently slip off two more complete folds. Again chain 2, then slip off two more folds.

This process is repeated until you have slipped off 12 complete folds, ending with 2 chains. (Where two strip ends are slipped off together, they count as one "fold".)

Look carefully at the folds you have worked off. If you separate the folds, you can see the crochet thread between them.

It is in this spot between folds that the crochet stitches will be made from this point forward in the rug—under the crochet thread that shows between each fold. Also from this point on, only double crochet stitches are used.

The rug is worked in a continuous spiral without chaining up between rounds.

To keep track of where the rounds begin, use a small safety pin to mark the beginning of each round. Move it up a row as you begin each new round. At the beginning of a round rug, put the safety pin into the very first fold that was worked off the hook.

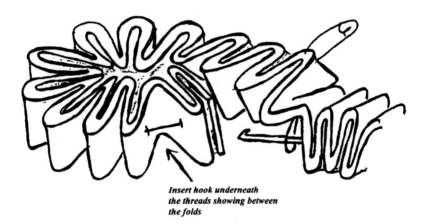

Insert hook underneath
the threads showing between
the folds

Second Round: Coil the first 12 folds to form a circle, with the side where the crochet thread shows to the inside. Make sure that the folds are not twisted.

In the space beyond the very first fold insert 1 double crochet stitch under the crochet thread in the folds. Gently work two folds of fabric off the end of the hook, pulling the crochet thread through them.

Page 123

The space after the next fold is where the next double crochet stitch will be inserted. Note that you can see the double crochet stitch that you just made. One fold of fabric should separate each of the double crochet stitches.

Insert a double crochet into the next space, then work off two more folds of fabric. The "*" instructions are repeated 12 times total, which will bring you around the center completing the second round. Move the safety pin up to the last fold in this round to mark the place.

Third Round: In every space between the folds, insert 1 double crochet and work off two folds of fabric. Move the safety pin to mark the last fold in this round.

"STRAIGHT" ROUNDS

Fourth and Fifth rounds: In every space between the folds, insert one double crochet and work off **ONE** fold of fabric. Remember to keep the pin marking the end of each round. These rounds are called "straight" rounds since there is one double crochet and one fold of fabric.

"INCREASE" ROUNDS

6th round: Double crochet in the first space and pull off **TWO** folds of fabric. Double crochet in the following space, and pull off **ONE** fold of fabric. Continue around **alternately working off two folds and one fold** with each double crochet stitch.

TO CONTINUE

The rug is completed by making several "Straight" rounds (see 4th and 5th round) followed by an "Increase" round (see 6th round). This is necessary for the rug to keep its shape and lay flat. Use a checklist to keep track of where you are so that you can be sure to get the increases in the proper places.

Beginning at the 7th round:
Make 2 straight rounds
    Make 1 increase round
Make 3 straight rounds
    Make 1 increase round
Make 5 straight rounds
    Make 1 increase round
Make 7 straight rounds
    Make 1 increase round
Make 9 straight rounds
    Make 1 increase round

You should notice a pattern in the "straight" rounds. They continue in a progression 3-5-7-9. The next step would be to make 11 straight rounds before the next increase round, then 13-15-17, etc. With this progression you can make a round rug as large as you like. But be sure to keep track of which round you have completed on a checklist.

The above increase pattern will keep a bent hook rug laying flat 90% of the time. If however, you notice that the rug is beginning to "cup" jump to the next increase row in the pattern. "Cupping" is most likely to occur when using heavy fabrics.

If you notice that you rug is beginning to wave, most likely you've made an extra increase round somewhere along the line. Don't let the waving get too pronounced before you correct it. To correct a wave, simply skip any increase rounds in the pattern until the edge lies flat again.

LAST ROUND

When the rug reaches the desired size, make one final round pulling off two folds of fabric with every double crochet stitch. This gives a full and solid edge finish.

When you have completed the final round and pulled off the last fold of fabric, slip stitch into the next space and pull up the end of the thread through the stitch to anchor it.

Cut the thread about six inches from the knot, and using a tapestry needle or similar, work the thread into the body of the rug, sewing back and forth to secure the thread. Clip off any excess thread.

OVAL RUGS

It is not difficult to adapt the round shape to make an oval rug with the bent hook method. Along the sides, you will always pull off one fold with each double crochet, just like the sample shirred project.

Think of the ends of the oval as half circles. The pattern of alternating straight and increase rows at these ends is exactly the same as for the round rug.

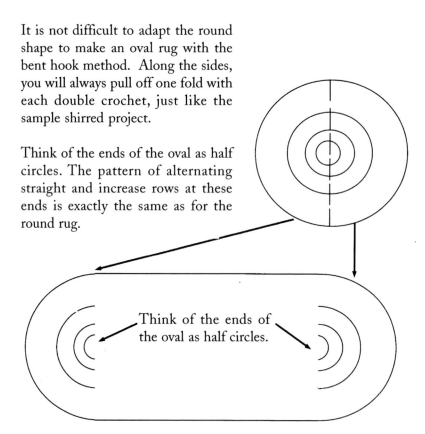

Think of the ends of the oval as half circles.

Follow the pattern of "increase" rounds only at the ends of an oval. Along the sides, there will always be only one fold pulled off the hook with each stitch which makes the sides of the oval the easiest place to create a pattern using counted folds.

Patterns can be worked along the sides of oval rugs at any time because all of the rows are "straight", but if you wish to make a continuous pattern all around the oval, plan to place the design in a long series of straight rows around the ends.

To begin an oval rug, create a base chain that is as long as the difference between the length and the width of the rug. For example, if the finished rug is planned to be five feet long and three feet wide, the difference between those measurements is two feet—the length of the base chain needed.

Have the hook fully loaded with fabric strip, with all ends trimmed evenly. Use a good quality, mercerize crochet thread, and make a slip knot on the hook.

Gently slip one fold off the end of the hook, pulling the slip knot through the fold.

With the thread, chain 2. Gently slip off the next fold. Again chain 2, then slip off the next fold. This process is repeated until the base chain reaches the desired length. (Where two strip ends are slipped off together, they count as one "fold".)

Look carefully at the folds you have worked off. Notice that on one side, the crochet thread shows, while on the other side it is hidden between the folds. While working back along the base chain, the crochet stitches will be made under the threads that are visible at the surface.

Turn the work, and slip off another two more folds of fabric. Then make a double crochet stitch in the second fold from the hook. Pull off a fold, double crochet in the next place. Repeat until you reach the end of the base chain.

Turn the work, chain two and pull off three folds of fabric. Mark the last fold with a small safety pin as this is the end of the first complete round and the beginning of the second.

From this point forward, all double crochet stitches will be worked in the spaces between the folds. Make a double crochet in between the first and second folds. Pull off a fold and double crochet into the next space. Repeat the procedure until you reach the end of the base.

Identify the three folds at the end. In the space before each of these folds, make a double crochet stitch and pull off **two folds** of fabric after each stitch.

Work back along the other straight side pulling off one fold between double crochet stitches. At the final end, repeat the process of pulling off two folds with each double crochet stitch in the space before each of the three end folds.

SIDES OF AN OVAL
These are always worked with one fold of fabric pulled off with each double crochet stitch.

ENDS OF AN OVAL
For the second complete round, make six stitches at the ends with two folds pulled off between the folds.
For the third complete round, make 12 stitches with two folds pulled off between the folds.
The fourth and fifth rounds are "straight" rounds, so even at the ends, only pull off one fold with each stitch.
The sixth round begins the pattern of "increase" rounds, made exactly like the round shape. Along the ends of the oval, alternate pulling off one fold, and then two folds as you crochet.
To continue, follow the same sequence of "straight" rounds and "increase" rounds given for the round rug. Of course, the "increase" pattern is only used through the curved portion at the ends of the rug.

SQUARE & RECTANGULAR RUGS IN ROUNDS

With square and rectangular rugs, there is no alternating of straight and increase rows. Instead, increases must be made in every row at each corner.

A square rug is begun the same as a round rug for the first 3 rounds. Then mark the corner placement with four small safety pins. As you reach the corner of the square, pull off three folds of fabric with the double crochet in the corner space. Repeat at every corner, in every round.

A rectangular rug is begun the same as the oval for the first three rounds. Then mark the four corners with small safety pins. As you reach the corner of the rectangle, pull off three folds of fabric with the double crochet in the corner space. Repeat at every corner in every round.

Patterns can be charted on square or rectangular rugs anywhere except in the corner spaces.

CROCHETING OCTAGONAL AND HEXAGONAL RUGS

These shapes are made by using pairs of double crochet stitches instead of using the technique for round rugs. If you are using lightweight wool, plan for a hexagon. If you are using heavy wool or shirring with multiple strips, plan for an octagon.

Hexagonal Rugs
Begin with a shirred chain of six folds and coil to a circle. Work between the folds and double crochet with one fold pulled off. Place two double crochet stitches in each space around for a total of 12 stitches. Mark the first pair of double-crochet stitches with a safety pin so that you know where each row will begin.

In the second round, work two double crochet (plus one fold) in the first fold, then work one double crochet in the next. The row continues alternating two stitches and one stitch in the folds around.

For the third round of stitching, a pair of double crochet stitches is worked in the first fold and just one stitch in each of the following two folds. That is repeated around the row.

Each following row will begin with a pair of double crochet stitches, followed by individual stitches that increase by one every time around. There will be three individual stitches in the next row, followed by four, then five, and so on. To preserve the hexagonal shape, make sure that you always begin the new row count with a pair of stitches.

Octagonal

Begin with a shirred chain of eight folds and coil to a circle. Work between the folds and double crochet with one fold pulled off. Place two double crochet stitches in each space around for a total of 16 stitches. Mark the first pair of double-crochet stitches with a safety pin so that you know where each row will begin.

In the second round, work two double crochet (plus one fold) in the first fold, then work one double crochet in the next. The row continues alternating two stitches and one stitch in the folds around.

For the third round of stitching, a pair of double crochet stitches is worked in the first fold and just one stitch in each of the following two folds. That is repeated around the row.

Each following row will begin with a pair of double crochet stitches, followed by individual stitches that increase by one every time around. There will be three individual stitches in the next row, followed by four, then five, and so on. To preserve the hexagonal shape, make sure that you always begin the new row count with a pair of stitches.

WORKING BACK AND FORTH IN ROWS

For a long, runner style rug, crocheted shirring can be worked back and forth in rows. This has the advantage of never needing to keep track of "increase" rows or pairs of stitches. Because every row has the same number of stitches and they are lined up, runner style rugs lend themselves to creating patterns with counted folds.

Begin by shirring a base chain of folds. The base chain can be either the desired width of the rug or the length of the rug.

For the first row of stitching, chain two and turn the work. Pull off one fold, skip the first fold space and insert the first double crochet stitch in the second. Pull off one fold. Continue along the row with one double-crochet (plus one fold) in each fold space. At the end of the row, repeat the above instructions. Note that the very first row of double crochet stitches is the most awkward since the stitches are worked on the "back" of the base chain. Following rows are worked between the folds.

ALTERNATIVE CROCHETING TECHNIQUES
Some people have difficulty making a double crochet stitch in the confined spaces between the folds of fabric. They will find it easier to substitute a single crochet stitch plus a chain stitch for the double crochet stitches.

If you tend to crochet very tightly, you may find that the folds bunch up. If you can't seem to loosen up, to allow the fabric to lay naturally, add an extra chain stitch after the double crochet (before you pull off the fold of fabric). Also if you are working with heavy wool, or doubling up wool for the shirring, you may need a little extra length in the stitch to accommodate the bulk of the fabric. In that case, add a chain stitch after each double crochet stitch.

For very light and/or flimsy fabrics, the rug surface may not be tight enough when a double crochet stitch is used. In that case, substitute a half-double or single crochet stitch in the pattern. For these types of fabrics, however, it really is best just to shir with two or more strips at the same time. See the Handbook section for more on using multiple strips.

CHAPTER 12

WORKING ROUND PATTERNS BY COUNTING FOLDS

Patterns can be worked into any of the crocheted shirred, sewn shirred or faux shirred rugs by counting folds of shirred fabric. These patterns work most easily with the crocheted techniques since the folds are evenly spaced.

Counted folds can be used to create simple geometric shapes in the parts of the rug that are not curved (along the sides of ovals, rectangles and squares) and in the "straight" rows of bent-hook shirring. Geometric forms with straight lines are the easiest, most often a simple cross was used covering just three rows of shirring for a small scale design.

For round rugs and the curved portions of ovals, geometrics with diagonal lines are most appropriate (diamonds, stars, etc.). The most common pattern worked into shirred rugs is the "Star" pattern, because it is so simple to do. The points of the star are made by decreasing the number of folds of the fabric which make up the star over seven rounds (or more) of shirring.

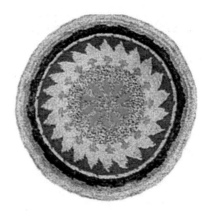

The temptation in creating patterns with counted folds is to overdo it. Rugs with too many small patterns can look busy (and dated) like this example from a "Rugbee" advertisement from the 1990s.

The technique of counting folds requires a little planning. Draw your design on graph paper with notes on how many folds are used in each row. Load the afghan hook or bent hook in the same order that the folds will be worked off, always shirring the folds onto the pointed end of the hook.

Patterns are easiest to re-create with the grid style of rug, but if you keep in mind that the "straight rows" of oval and rectangular rugs are also the same construction as the grid, it is easier to plan for the rug design.

Most often in older round and oval rugs, patterns were very simple, usually with a center of a single color (or hit-or-miss rows) followed by an edge of several points that gave the entire rug the look of a star. The chart below shows a simple progression forming a point that can be used as a border around a round rug.

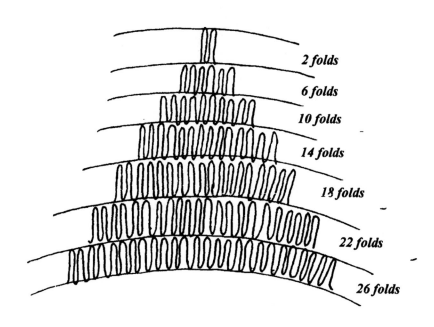

2 folds

6 folds

10 folds

14 folds

18 folds

22 folds

26 folds

CHAPTER 13

EDGE SHIRRING

Edge shirring creates a more complex texture than center shirring, and even though it is not any harder to do, the rugs seem to impress people more. The process of shirring with needle and thread is the same whether you are making a center shirred rug or an edge shirred rug. The difference lies only in the placement of the stitching line. Edge shirred rugs are not reversible. They will have one side with the fullness of the shirring and the back side will have a tight, flat surface.

FABRICS

Almost any fabric can be used for edge shirred rugs. Light fabrics will form a dense pile while heavy resilient fabrics will emphasize the shirred texture. Light woven cottons will pack down in use, but other fabrics, including knits, woolens, fleece and synthetics will retain softness underfoot. Most commonly edge shirred rugs are made with heavy wool, often from recycled coats, but they are certainly adaptable to all sorts of recycled fabrics.

Since edge shirring has more bulk along the edge that is not stitched, the shirring will form a naturally mounded shape by itself, making it ideal for pillows and chairpads. To create a rug that lays flat, "spacing" strips are required between each round of shirring. These spacing strips can be of folded fabric, center-shirred fabric, cording or braids. By using contrasting colors for the shirring and spacing strips visual depth is added to the rug.

Basic Edge Shirring for Pillows and Chairpads

Since pillows and chairpads aren't subject to heavy wear, almost any fabric can be used and the fabric strips can be cut wider than for rugs. The shirring will develop a hollow in the back which can be filled with polyfil, a pillow form or foam.

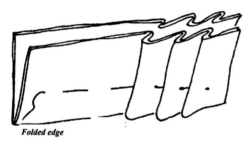

Folded edge

For heavy fabrics (coat or blanket wool or polar fleece) cut strips 1.5 to 2 inches wide. These are shirred one strip at a time. Lighter fabrics can be shirred using two strips together, or they can be cut twice as wide, folded in half and shirred along the fold as illustrated at the left.

Woven fabrics should be cut on the bias. Square off the ends of the strip before shirring. See the Handbook section for preparing other fabrics.

A 14-inch pillow will require about a yard of heavy fabrics (two yards of lighter fabrics) or one large sweater or sweatshirt.

DIRECTIONS:

1. Cut a length of linen thread, mercerized crochet cotton or heavy duty carpet thread five to six feet long, and thread a long embroidery

or shirring needle. Knot the thread ends together to form a double strand.

2. Insert the needle ¼-inch from the edge and ¼-inch from the end of the strip, then pass the needle through the thread loop and pull it up snug. This anchors the end of the thread before you begin shirring.

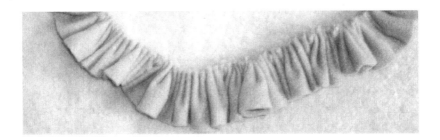

3. The shirring stitch is simply the running stitch, bringing the needle in and out of the strip at about ½-inch intervals. The line of stitching is placed ¼-inch from the edge of the strip.

Shir several strips, pushing them down along the thread so that they are packed firmly but not so tightly that the folds are forced to twist around the thread. When you have just enough thread left to conveniently end the thread, knot it off and begin a new thread. Pass the new thread through several folds of the already shirred strip.

4. When three or four feet of shirring complete, you can begin the project assembly. Use the same type of thread as that for the shirring. Have the needle threaded with a doubled length of thread and knotted.

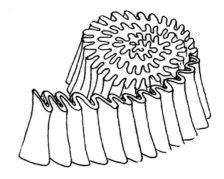

Note that in the assembly, stitches are placed along the shirring line, so hold the strip with the shirred edge facing up.

Roll the shirring into a snug, round coil to a size that can be conveniently held in your left hand (lefties reverse this). Make sure that the shirred edges all line up in the coil. Stitch through the center coil (at the shirring line) several times to make sure it is very firmly held.

The shirred strip is then stitched around this center coil, making sure always that the edges of the shirred strips are aligned. The figure eight stitch is used to assemble edge shirring. (This is exactly the same stitching as sewn center shirring.)

Insert the needle about ¼-inch from the edge of the strip, and push it into the work so that it comes out at least two rows of shirring toward the center. Pull up the thread. Insert the needle slightly in the same where the thread comes out, angling the needle so that it will emerge about ½-inch from where the stitch began. Pull up the thread.

Make the next stitch inserting the needle near of where the thread emerges from the rug so that the needle passes through at least two rows of shirring. Pull up the thread. Continue stitching, knotting off and beginning a new thread as needed. All knots should be placed between the folds of the shirring.

After only a few rounds of sewing,

you'll notice the work start to mound up in the center. If you notice that the mounding is too extreme, you will need to add a spacing strip (see the next section). This can happen if you cut the strips for edge shirring wider than an inch of a "springy" fabric, like polar fleece.

Ending. Edge shirring can be ended at any point when used without spacing strips. When completed, the outside rows of shirring will lay out away from the pillow and the center will bound up creating a hollow in the back. This hollow is filled with a round pillow form or polyester fill, and then back the piece with a matching fabric. You can end a chair pad by adding tie-backs if desired.

EDGE SHIRRING WITH SPACING STRIPS

To make an edge shirred rug that lays flat, you have to overcome the tendency of the shirring to form a mound. This is done by placing spacing strips between rows of shirring as the rug is assembled, which allows the upper (unshirred) edge of the strip the room it needs to expand to cover the surface of the rug.

Cut the strips for shirring on the bias, using heavy blanket wool or other woven fabrics. Nonwoven fabrics can be cut in any direction. Strips are usually cut 1.5 inches wide, but not less than 1 inch. These spacing strips are used folded in half or thirds. In order to keep the rug laying flat, the spacing strips have to be just as thick as the base of the edge shirring.

Estimating yardage. For edge shirred rugs you will need about 1 yard of 60-inch wide wool (or about two pounds of recycled or scrap wool) for each square foot of finished rug. A wool coat will yield about three pounds of usable wool, so for a rug with six square feet, you will need four coats. (Note that these are estimated yardages. Less fabric will be required with very heavy or stiff wool; more fabric will be required for lighter or more loosely woven fabrics.) You can make a small rug with four or five recycled sweaters.

DIRECTIONS

The edge shirring proceeds in exactly the same manner as for the chair pad. The difference comes with the assembly. To assemble an edge shirred rug with spacing strips, stitch both strips directly to the rug. The sewing is done alternately.

Use a long needle threaded with a double length and knotted. Begin by coiling the shirred section for two or three rounds, then stitch through it several times using a figure eight stitch. (For an oval, fold over the shirred strip and begin stitching at the fold.)

Once the center is formed, lay the folded spacing strip in place so that the edges line up with the shirred edge of the center. Begin stitching the spacing strip to the shirred center. Make sure that you are stitching in the same direction as the center is coiled. When the spacing strip is stitched around, change back to sewing the shirred section.

The assembly continues in this same manner, alternately stitching the shirring and the spacer to the rug. At the outside, make one or two complete rounds with just the shirring (no spacing strip) so that the shirring will lie flat to the floor and hide the stitching lines.

CREATING INTEREST WITH THE SPACING STRIP

There are several options, besides simply folding the spacing strip, which can create design interest in the rug. A favorite of mine is to use a 3-strand braid, made of lighter weight wool in colors that coordinate with the shirring. The braid is used on the edge (not flat) so that a striped effect is achieved in the spacing. Also tubes of wool can be sewn and turned inside out for the spacing strips.

DOUBLE SHIRRING

The most interesting texture of all is to use ½- to ¾-inch strips of lightweight wool which have been *center* shirred as the spacing strips. This double shirring is the most time consuming of the spacing options, but it is the easiest way to make sure that the rug lays flat and it creates the richest look even with recycled fabrics.

CHAPTER 14

MONO-SHIRRING

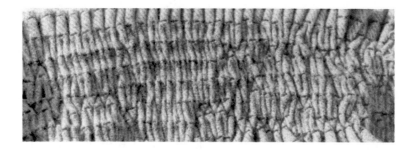

The mono-shirred rug is unique in that it begins with one large piece of fabric, not fabric strips. The fabric is gathered up with running stitches to give it depth and softness for a rug. Traditionally mono-shirred rugs were made from blankets that had worn thin, and were used mostly as bedside rugs, sometimes being re-dyed to match different color schemes.

Modern mono-shirred rugs are most often made using wool yard goods or blankets, but many other fabrics, including stretch fabrics will make quite attractive rugs. Almost any medium to heavy weight cloth is suitable for this type of rug making. (Heavy fabrics will make a larger rug compared to medium weight fabrics of the same size.) Used blankets, fleece or flannel sheets are also good choices but do not try to use small pieces of fabric from recycled clothing.

When selecting a fabric for mono-shirring, especially for your first rug, choose a plaid or a fabric with stripes or a linear print running the length of the goods, since these markings can be used to guide your stitches. On solid color fabrics and large prints you will have to mark all of the sewing lines. This can be and time-consuming.

For your first project use a piece of cloth that is wide enough to make the rug in a single section. On later projects, you may want to join several pieces of cloth together to reach the size or design you have in mind. For mono-shirred rugs, heavy fabrics are butted together (sewn edge to edge so that there is not a thick seam).

The process of mono-shirring is begun by determining the size of the rug you want to make. The **width** of the fabric is the **length** of the finished rug. The length of the fabric is roughly eight times the width of the finished rug.

It is easiest to use yard goods that are made in the desired width for the size of your rug. Most wool fabric is available in 54- to 60-inch widths which is usually long enough for accent rugs. Since the selvage edges are already finished, they will not ravel and do not require any attention before shirring is begun.

If you are using a blanket and wish to cut it down to a smaller size, it may be necessary to stitch along the edges to keep them from raveling. Traditionally the edges are handsewn with a blanket stitch, though a zigzag stitch on a sewing machine will do a satisfactory job.

For an example of how to calculate how much yardage you will need for a mono-shirred rug with a medium weight wool. For a rug three feet wide and five feet long, the width of the yard goods at 60 inches (five feet) will be the length of the rug. To have a width of three feet when shirred, you will need 24 feet of fabric (8 x 3 = 24). Twenty-four feet is equal to eight yards of fabric.

DIRECTIONS

1. Cut a strip 3 inches wide from each end of the fabric, making sure that your cutting line is straight across the with of the goods. (Follow a line of the plaid or print.) These strips will be used in the finishing and this step also makes sure that you have a straight edge of fabric at the beginning and the end of the shirred section.

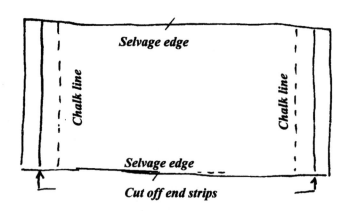

Selvage edge

Chalk line

Chalk line

Selvage edge

Cut off end strips

2. Draw a chalk line straight across the goods, two to three inches in from the edge just cut, at both ends of the fabric. These are the beginning and ending lines of the shirring. The extra fabric will be folded up when the shirring is finished to hide the knots of the shirring threads.

3. Cut a length of the shirring thread that is twice the width of the rug plus a couple of feet for adjustments and knotting. The thread is used doubled, so knot the ends together, leaving at least two inches of thread after the knot. (It is always better to have the thread a bit too long than too short.

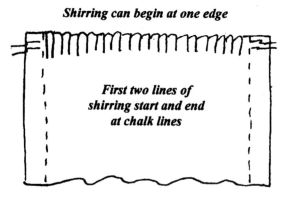

Shirring can begin at one edge

First two lines of shirring start and end at chalk lines

4. Begin shirring. Your first line of shirring can be along either selvage edge, or you can begin at the center and work out to the edges. (If you are not using a plaid or stripe, you will need to mark your stitching lines one inch apart, all along the fabric.)

Shirring can begin at the center

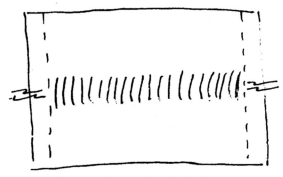

Do not shir past the chalk lines

Take the first running stitch by inserting the needle at the chalk line, near the selvage, and bring it out 1/2 inch away. Follow a plaid line to make sure that your stitching line is straight. Continue taking your running stitches along the line until you reach the other end of the fabric.

When you finish this line of shirring, clip the thread just below the needle, and knot the thread ends together, leaving at least two inches of thread beyond the knot. DO NOT PULL THE SHIRRING UP TIGHTLY. The shirring should be loose so that you can make the next line of stitching.

5. Shir the entire width of the rug, following the same procedure as for the first line of stitching. Place your stitching lines one inch apart, and try to line up your stitches with the previous row of stitching. Remember that a new thread is used for each row.

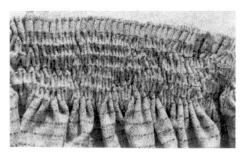

6. After all of the stitching is complete, you will begin to actually shape the rug. At the first end, find the thread ends of the first two rows of stitching. Pull them up just enough to see the knots. Tie these two thread sections together so that the new knot is between the old knots and the shirring.

Work across the rug, tying these threads together in pairs. If you do not have an even number of threads, knot three threads together in the middle of the rug, not at an edge.

7. When all of the knots are tied at the first end, you will begin to pull up the shirring at the other end of the rug. Work on a flat surface.

Take two stitching threads at a time, hold them securely and push the shirring down along the threads until the shirring is firm, but not so tight as to strain the threads. Work along the entire end until all threads are pulled up snugly.

Have a yardstick handy to measure the rug width so that as you tie the knots on this end, the shirred section stays the same width. Knot the first pair of threads together, firmly holding the shirring in place.

Measure the width of the shirring. Knot the next pair, and measure again to make sure that the shirring width is the same. Continue along this edge knotting and measuring until the entire rug is securely tied. Double check your measurements to make sure that the shirred width is even. Re-tie any knots necessary.

End flaps folded over to hide knots.
Sew in place.

8. Finishing. When all of the knots are tied and even, you are ready to fold up the end flaps of fabric to cover the knots. Tuck under the raw edge and stitch the flap in place.

Finally, using the two strips of fabric that you cut off at the very beginning, you can cover the shirred edges. (If the selvages look neat enough, you can skip this step.) Pin the strip to the edge of the rug, and tuck under the raw edge of the strip. Use backstitches to secure the strip on both sides of the rug. The rug is now completed. You may wish to steam the end flaps to make them lay flat.

CARING FOR A MONO-SHIRRED RUG

If you lightly vacuum (suction only) and turn the rug regularly, an annual dry cleaning is usually all that is necessary. (For washable rugs, such as those made from acrylic blankets, use the gentle washing machine cycle and lay the rug flat to dry.)

One problem peculiar to mono-shirred rugs is that over several years, the shirring may "flatten out" creating a hard or thin spot. This can happen if the shirring threads stretch and is a problem when cotton threads are used for the shirring. This can easily be solved by opening up one end flap and retying the knots to tighten up the rug again. Most often once the knots are retied, the rug will not flatten out again since all of the stretch has been taken out of the threads.

CHAPTER 15

COMBINATION RUGS

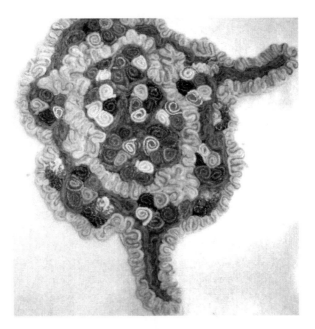

The techniques of shirring and standing wool rugs can be combined in many different ways. For example, the spacing strips used with edge shirred rugs are used in the same way as the strips for standing wool rugs. Sewn center shirring is also discussed as a decorative type of spacing strip for edge shirred rugs. However, when combining shirring and standing wool, the possibilities are much greater than simply alternating the two kinds of strips in the rug surface.

Combination rugs have an unlimited potential for free form art rugs and wall hangings. Shirred wool, "beads" of wool and lines of standing wool can be stitched together in an orderly design, or randomly for an overall effect rich in textural variation. Even small wall hangings can have a very large visual impact, so it is the combinations of these techniques that are really the most fun of all.

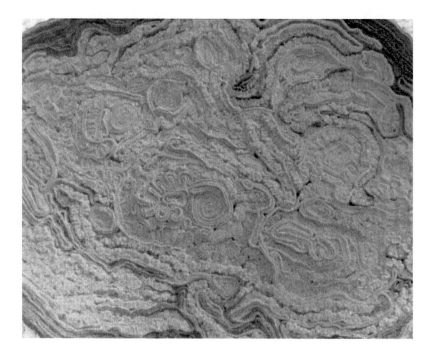

The combination rug above is entitled "Fire Agate" and is shown in color on the back cover. This image emphasizes the textures of the design. The free form shape takes advantage of the potential for design in both shirring and standing wool. Note the way in which the two textures combine to accent each other, and how the freeform construction gives the rug an organic feel. Freeform rugs are really where the textile artist has the greatest freedom for exploring texture and color in shirred and standing wool rugs.

PART 2

HANDBOOK

FOR SHIRRED &

STANDING WOOL RUGS

THREADS

If you had x-ray vision and looked down on a shirred or standing wool rug, you would see a spider web of threads or crochet stitches. It is the thread which holds these rugs together. Throughout the individual chapters, a good quality mercerized cotton crochet thread is recommended. The brand that I've used for many years is the DMC Baroque cotton which is super-mercerized. If you can't find that, an easy way to tell if a thread is strong enough for these rugs is to simply pull it to see how easily it breaks. Crochet threads, upholstery threads, carpet threads, buttonhole thread, etc., are all perfectly suitable. Avoid the 4-ply cotton rug warp and other threads that aren't tightly spun.

NEEDLES AND HOOKS

For the sewn varieties of standing wool, center shirring and faux shirring, you'll want as long a needle as you can find. Some embroidery needles are three inches long and they will certainly work. Needles marketed for soft scupture and doll making are better since they are five or six inches long. For most applications a blunt tip is much better than a pointed tip. Not only do you spare your fingers lots of stab wounds, a blunt tip is also better for working between strands in the fabrics rather than cutting or splitting them. The exception is with hard to penetrate fabrics like denim, where a pointed tip is a better choice.

FABRICS

Shirred rugs can be made of almost any fabric or recycled clothing. Because the techniques can use tiny pieces of fabric, they are also ideal for using up scraps.

The traditional material for these rugs is wool, but very attractive rugs can be made of cottons, blends, and even knit fabrics. If you're making an art piece that will be hung on the wall, you can use absolutely any fabric or ribbon. But if you're making a rug, you will want to select a fabric that has resilience so that the rug holds its shape and has some "give" underfoot. For rugs, avoid light quilting cottons and calicos, as they will pack down in use resulting in a hard mat, not a soft rug.

Not all fabrics work equally well with every shirring or standing wool method. For example, denim seems to work fine with crocheted shirring, but will pack to a solid mat with sewn shirring or standing wool techniques. Additionally, the weave of a fabric will affect its appearance in the rug.

Heavy wool (blankets, coats, meltons and felted wool) are best suited to standing wool rugs, and sewn center shirring, edge shirring and faux shirring. They are usually too tightly woven to use easily with a crochet hook, but if you don't mind the extra effort, crocheted shirring can be done with them (use a Size 8 steel hook). These heavy fabrics are also ideal for mono-shirring.

Medium to light woolens work well with all of the center shirring methods and faux shirring, and they can be used in a double or triple thicknesses heavier rugs. Woolens with a more open weave make a very soft rug with a velvety finish.

Fleece can be used in many shirring techniques. The heaviest polar fleece will also work in standing wool rugs and mono-shirring. Clothing weight fleece is usually easier to handle with shirring, since heavy fleece is often resistant to a sewing needle. Even though I prefer using a blunt tipped needle for shirring in general, for fleece a sharp pointed needle is usually necessary.

Knit fabrics (synthetic or cotton) work best with the crocheted shirring techniques, but heavy sweaters can be used for sewn center shirring, and wool sweaters that have been shrunk and tightened can be used for beaded rugs.

Feel free to experiment any sort of fabric. I've made wonderful rugs from open-weave draperies, bedspreads and old jeans. You can also combine various types of fabric in the same rug if you're careful in laundering it. Many light fabrics which can't be used for other types of rug making work very nicely for shirred rugs. Even lightweight open-weave fabrics create a rug surface with a luxurious softness because the edge threads will "open up" as the rug is used.

ESTIMATING YARDAGES
FOR SHIRRED & STANDING WOOL RUGS
FOR EACH SQUARE FOOT OF RUG,
ALLOW THE YARDAGE SHOWN OF 45-INCH WIDE
FABRICS

FABRIC WEIGHT	1/2" strips	3/4" strips	1" strips	1.5" strips
LIGHT	3/4 yd	1 yd	1-1/2 yd	2-1/4 yd
MEDIUM	1/2 yd	3/4 yd	1 yd	1-1/2 yd
HEAVY	3/8 yd	1/2 yd	3/4 yd	1-1/8 yd

GENERAL GUIDELINES FOR
FABRIC PREPARATION

In most cases, the width of the fabric strips that you cut will be the thickness of your finished rug. For instance, if you cut your strips one inch wide, your rug will be one inch thick. (Very light fabrics and very loosely woven fabrics will make a finished rug that is a bit thinner than the strip since these types of fabrics "give" at the edge.)

For all types of shirred rugs **except edge shirring**, rugs can be made successfully from strips from 1/2 inch to 1-1/2 inches wide. Of course all of the strips for the particular rug should all be the same width, so choose one for the thickness of your rug, unless you are creating a special effect in the rug, such as "sculpting."

A little practice cutting will allow you to make strips that are generally even, so do not get discouraged on your first cut. Each strip will probably have wider and narrower places. In the finished rug, overly wide strip sections will stick up above the surface and can be clipped off to even the surface. If you cut a section of strip that is unacceptably narrow, just discard that section and shir with the remainder.

A QUICK GUIDE TO STRIP WIDTH

For heavy wools, fleeces, denim and similar heavy fabrics, choose a strip width **between 1/2 and 1 inch.**

For medium weight fabrics choose a strip width between **3/4 and 1-1/4 inches.**

For light fabrics choose a strip width between **3/4 and 1-1/2 inches.**

Of course for rugs used in traffic areas, thinner rugs are more appropriate. Lounging rugs, such as in front of a fireplace can be thicker, but they also should have their edges tapered to minimize the hazard of tripping.

CUTTING KNIT FABRICS

As a general rule, knit fabrics should be cut in the direction with the least amount of stretch. In most knits, this will be across the rows of knitting, vertically on garments, and parallel to the selvage edge in new fabrics.

CUTTING FELTED AND SIMILAR NON-WOVEN FABRICS

These fabrics do not have a "grain" so they can be cut in any direction.

CUTTING WOVEN FABRICS

Unlike most other hand made rugs, the fabric strips for shirred and standing wool rugs are cut on the bias of the fabric. Cutting on the bias is not as difficult as it may seem.

Actually on some fabrics the most confusing part is locating the straight grain. (If you are working on a difficult fabric, it may be necessary to clip and tear the fabric to find the straight grain.)

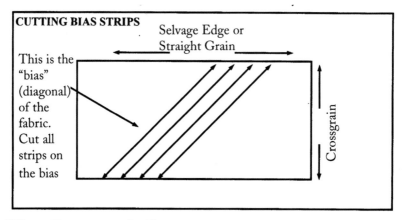

CUTTING BIAS STRIPS

Selvage Edge or Straight Grain

This is the "bias" (diagonal) of the fabric. Cut all strips on the bias

Crossgrain

When Cutting on the Bias

Most fabrics for used for shirred and standing wool rugs will need to be cut on the bias. With new fabrics, you can identify the bias by simply folding the end of the fabric over to the selvage edge. With fabric recycled from clothing, the straight grain can be found by clipping and tearing along a thread (so the bias is at a 45-degree diagonal to the tear).

You can use scissors to cut bias strips, but a roller knife and cutting mat is by far the quickest. I have found that when cutting wool, even heavy melton wool, that the fabric will stretch and distort with the pressure of the roller knife. The best solution is to use wool pieces that are less than 15 inches wide. Twelve inches has become my standard over the years. The bias cuts are short enough that the stretch in the cutting process is minimal.

FABRIC APPEARANCE

Both shirred and standing wool rugs show only the cut edge of a fabric, and the appearance of a fabric surface can be very different than how it will look in a shirred rug. Overall plaids, stripes and houndstooth will create a fairly uniformly speckled background.

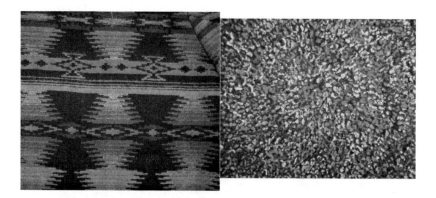

Boldly patterned wool will create a heathered effect in which all of the surface colors are randomly represented. Above is a photo of the same shirred rug shown on the back cover in color. The wool from which it was made is on the left. If you want to create a similar "heathered" look, select a wool that looks the same on both sides. Cut the fabric into one-foot sections and then cut the bias strips from those sections.

Brocades, jacquards and other patterned weaves which appear in reversed colors from front to back will not result in a heathered effect. Instead the threads used in the weave will appear in the same

proportion as they appear in the weave, resulting in a completely different blended color. Above is an example of a brocade, woven in a light blue and gold (recycled drapes). When cut on the bias and shirred, the rug surface is a blend of the two colors, in this case a pale green.

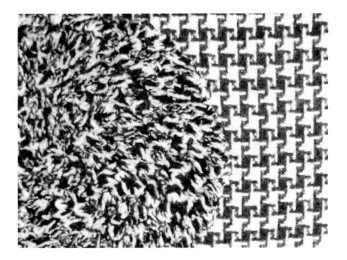

Twills and houndstooth wovens that have bold contrast in the threads will result in a "frosted" appearance, like the traditional Snow-on-the-Mountain sample above. The larger the thread size, the more pronounced the effect. It doesn't matter which technique you use for a shirred rug, the appearance of these types of fabrics is consistent.

By contrast, twills with little contrast (above) and small plaids and plaids with lots of colored threads (below) will make a shirred rug with one combined tone, when viewed from "rug distance."

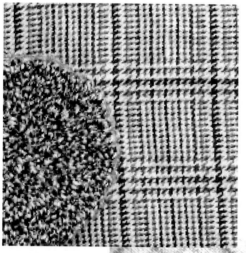

These fabrics make good backgrounds for patterns with counted folds.

Finely woven, lightweight wool plaids will develop the smoothest, most evenly toned surface in shirred rugs.

Combining two different small plaids will create more visual interest "almost" like the h e a t h e r i n g effect in boldly woven wools.

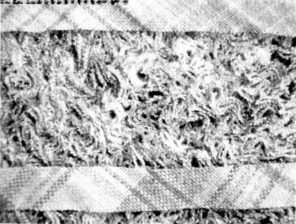

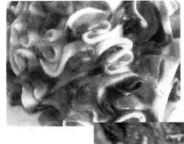

Heavy melton wool, polar fleece (left) and handmade felt (below) all show a prominent edge in shirred rugs.

Use those of types of fabrics to emphasize the texture of the rug, shape of the folds and bold design elements.

Fabrics with an open weave, even a loose weave, can be successfully used for shirred rugs of all varieties. Loosely woven fabrics should be cut not less than one inch (and on the bias, of course).

In this example a loosely woven c o t t o n bedspread was recycled. The result is a soft, chenille-type surface.

Fabrics in solid colors will not change shades of course, but the type of weave will determine how the rug looks. Shirting and skirt wools of a slightly open weave (not wool flannel) will make very plush surfaces on shirred rugs. (Years ago, I'd made one of red

shirting wool and a woman asked how I'd made velvet that thick. These fabrics are the ones to choose for that velvety texture.)

Some woven cotton fabrics will also appear velvety including corduroy and denim. (Old blue jeans create a light blue velveteen look.) The cotton fabrics, however, should be worked with one of the crocheted shirring (or faux shirring) methods to keep the folds evenly spaced and the surface of the rug uniformly soft.

Sweaters are also good candidates for recycling, even synthetic sweaters with a fairly large stitch size.

Fine knits (at right) make soft, durable rugs and show the shirring stitches distinctly.

Cotton sweaters produce a chenille-like surface, just like open-weave cottons.

Synthetic sweaters will look more like shag carpeting with the individual yarn ends being visible.

T-shirts and sweatshirts act just like other fine knits for rugs. With t-shirts, it's a good idea to use two or more strips together in the shirring to give the rug a little more body.

There really are very few fabrics that can't be used for shirred and standing wool rugs. Quilting cotton will pack down when used by itself so it isn't a good choice. Also, be cautions of "craft felt" since some of it is really not strong enough or durable in rugs. To test for rug quality, wash the felt in hot, soapy water. If it tightens up and thickens, it is good quality. If it falls apart, save it for craft projects but don't use it for rugs.

Using Multiple Strips and Combining Different Weights of Fabric

After so many years of playing around with various shirring methods, I have to retract some advice given in the earlier editions. Shirred rugs of all types can be made with multiple strips used together without any loss in appearance or softness. Using multiple strips also saves time in the rug construction since each stitch is a little wider, so the rug grows more quickly.

By using strips of two different colors or shades in shirring, marvelous blendings, shadings and heathering can develop that just don't happen otherwise. The other bonus of using multiple strips is that you can combine woolens of different weights in the same rug and still maintain an even appearance in each row. You just have to pay attention to the combined thickness of the strips, adjusting the doubled or tripled strips to the same thickness as the heaviest wool that you plan to use in the rug.

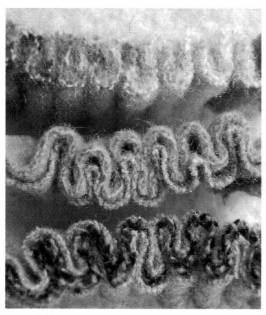

For example, if the heaviest wool you have on hand is a blanket weight wool (top row), it can be shirred as a single strip to use as a gauge.

A melton (coat weight) and a skirt weight wool can be used doubled to create stitches of about the same (middle row). Light suiting or skirt weight wool can be used tripled to acheive about the same size (bottom row).

How to Recycle Common Types of Clothing for Rugs

In general, with all types of clothing, make sure that it has been recently washed. Remove all buttons, pockets, belts, etc. Considering the price of wool, with wool coats, use a seam ripper to open the seams so you can obtain the maximum amount of usable wool. With other types of clothing, it is easier just to cut off the seams.

Recycling T-shirts and Sweatshirts

All cotton knits are handled in the same way.
1. Cut off all hems, seams and collars. Cut open all seams.

2. Cut strips straight up the lines of knitting. For most commerically produced garments, this will be vertical on the shirt, from hem to collar as illustrated.

3. Cut the sleeves from cuff to shoulder. If the shirt has long sleeves, and the elbows show signifcant wear, discard the worn sections.

If the shirt has a rubberized decoration, do not use that section for rug strips. They will be stiffer and harder than the rest of the rug. Save the rubberized section for some other craft project.

Recycling Cotton or Synthetic Sweaters

These can be used for wonderfully decorative rugs. The knitting yarns show at the edge of the strips. Everyone's first question is "Won't they unravel?" The answer is no, for a couple of reasons. First, knitting only ravels in one direction (from the top of the sweater) so it is only that end that could possible unravel. With the first shirring stitch through the strip, any ravelling would be stopped. Second, even if you tried to unravel a strip, you would have to intentionally pull out each short little piece of yarn. (With large knitted stitches, this is possible, especially if you have little ones with very busy hands, so just keep that in mind.)

You can use any sort of knitted sweater, hat or scarf and the type of knitting doesn't really matter, except as it can affect the bulk of the cut strip. The sweater shown above has only hems and a collar to remove, so it can be cut just like a t-shirt or sweatshirt. Below is a sweater with rib knit cuffs and hem. This tighter knitting has to be cut off before you cut strips from the sweater itself. Of course, you'll also cut off the collar and cut open the seams.

The cuffs and hem strips can be cut separately to the same width and used as a border in the rug.

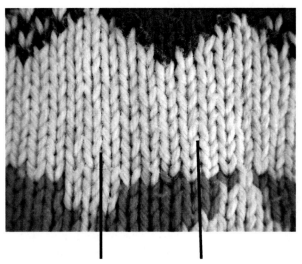

With finely knitted sweaters, the strips can be cut to any desired width (3/4-inch is good).

With more loosely knitted sweaters, the cutting has to be done more carefully.

Strips need to be cut straight up the line of knit stitches, and there must be **at least five complete stitches** in each strip, as illustrated.

Recycling Wool Sweaters

Wool is an ideal fabric for rugs, and wool sweaters make wonderful rugs, especially if they have been washed in hot water and dried in a hot dryer to shrink and "full" them. (Yes, I know the crafters call it "felting" but the proper textile term is "fulling.") Remove hems, or rib knit edges and cuffs, and collars. Cut open all seams.

Wool sweaters are cut into strips vertically, like other knits, just as a safety factor against potential ravelling since some sweater wool will resist fulling. Heavier sweaters can be used for standing wool rugs, including beaded rugs and lighter sweaters for all types of shirred rugs.

Recycling Socks

Yes, even those old socks can be recycled into rugs. Because we live in the far north, wool socks get heavy use, so we have a lot of them to recycle. This procedure will also work with cotton or synthetics.

To prepare socks, cut off the toe seam and then cut down the sock from the cuff to the toe, passing right through the heel, since that is usually where it has worn out. Cut across the sock to separate the rib knit part of the cuff from the rest of the plain knit.

Cut the sock parts vertically into strips of the same width. Keep the plain kit and rib knit strips separate, since they will have different bulk.

You can make any type of shirred rug from recycled socks, but do the shirring in sections. Begin by using only one type of strip (either all of the rib knit first, or all of the plain knit).

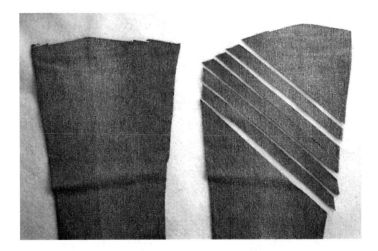

Recycling Old Jeans
One of the most often asked questions is from people who have saved old jeans hoping to make a rug from them. Shirred rugs from old jeans are the showiest rugs from denim since the shirred surface takes on the appearance of a light blue velveteen, which gets softer as the rug gets used and washed. You can use stretch denim, but classic heavy jean denim makes the best rugs.

Having said that, also note that I do not recommend using denim for you first shirred rug. The fabric is hard to penetrate with either a hook or a needle and will frustrate a new rug maker. Once you've made shirred rugs from an easier fabric, try out a little denim to see if you really want to use it.

To prepare old jeans for recycling, cut off hems, waistband and pockets. Discard the really worn sections around the knee, and if the jeans have a reinforced knee, discard those too. Cut 3/4-inch strips on the bias.

Note that these rugs get extremely heavy when wet and will be a problem to wash in a home washing machine. Instead use a commercial double- or triple-load machine at a laundromat and wash the rugs with other heavy items to balance the load.

At the left is a sample of the rib knit strips from one sock of the pair. Notice how the color of the sock band appears as speckles in the shirring.

Sculpting the Edge of a Shirred or Standing Wool Rug

OK, so you love the luxurious, soft feel of the shirred rug and you cut your strips an inch or more wide making it extra deep and soft. But lay that thick of a rug on the floor and people won't be stepping on it; they'll be tripping over it. The solution is to sculpt the edges of the rug.

Basic sculpting is done by gradually decreasing the width of the strip that you use for the outer edges of the rug. When the rug is just an inch or so smaller than you want the finished rug to be, it is time to start sculpting.

Cut strips ¼ inch narrower than the rest of the rug. You will need enough strip to work at least twice completely around the outside edge. For example, if your regular rug strips were one inch wide, you should cut these sculpting strips ¾ inch wide.

If you used heavy fabrics, a ¾ inch edge can still be a hazard to foot traffic, so repeat the process working at least two complete rounds with strips that are ½ inch wide. This process of tapering the edge should be used on any rug that is in use.

If you are using heavy wools or other heavy fabrics the edge should be tapered down a ¼ inch at a time until you have a ½-inch edge. For medium to light fabrics, taper the edge (a ¼ inch at a time) until the outside edge is ¾ inch thick.

When shirring the narrower sculpting strips, remember to work the shirring stitches and the assembling stitches in the **center** of the strip. The rows will flop over whichever way the rug lays when you turn over the rug, so don't worry that the rug won't lay flat.

If you want a more gradual slope to the tapered edge, just work more rounds of each of the narrower sculpting strips.

Creating Special Design Effects with Sculpting

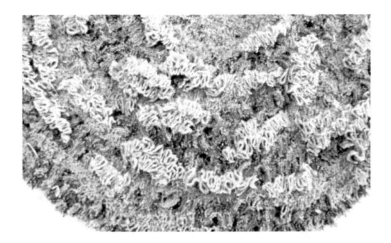

Sculpting shirred rugs has lots of possibilities. You can use it to accent a design in the rug, or you can 'sculpt' a pillow. These are just a couple of the possibilities. (Standing wool rugs can be accented with sculpting as well).

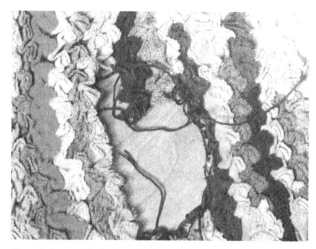

*Photo courtesy of
Joan Pachuta*

Repairing a Hole in a Shirred Rug

While this edition was in process, a lady named Joan Pachuta wrote asking how to repair a hole that her puppy had chewed in her shirred rug. Since accidents do happen, I thought I'd include the repair instructions here.

If there are loose thread ends in the hole, they need to be secured at the earliest opportunity to keep the damage from getting worse. Especially with crocheted shirring, the stitches can unravel. If the ends are long enough, tie knots in them—ideally tying two strings together. If the ends are too short to tie, use a good quality permanent fabric glue that is both flexible and washable and glue the ends of the string to the remaining shirred folds. The string ends should not stick up above the surface of the shirring.

To create a patch, use the same type of fabric in a matching shade, cut to the same width as the other strips in the rug. The patch is created one row at a time, using the Snow-on-the-Mountain technique in Chapter 9. Crochet a shirred chain that will exactly fit in one edge of the hole and sew it in place. Be sure to secure the ends of the shirred chain as well as the sides. Repeat for each row of shirring until the hole is completely filled in.

If only the fabric is gone and the string remains in the hole, you will need to clip and tie the strings around the edges of the hole so that you have "clean" sides to attach the patching shirred sections.

Making Your Own Non-Skid Mat

If you have polished floors, you'll need a non-skid mat to use under a shirred or standing wool rug. Because of the nature of these rugs, the expanded rubber mats sold for the purpose don't work too well. But you can make your own. The best mats for these rugs are actually other rugs. Find a thin el-cheapo bath mat or runner at a discount store to use. Cut it to size if needed.

If you are a hard-core recycler: remember when recycling t-shirts with large rubberized motifs that the rubberized area couldn't be used for the rug? Well, save several of those, stitch them together and lay them rubber side down to form the mat for your rug.

Caring for a Shirred or Standing Wool Rug

Shirred and standing wool rugs don't need a lot of special care to last for generations. There are only a couple of major cautions. Don't let the rug sit around where it will get wet on a regular basis. Too much repeated wetting may rot the warp threads. Don't store the rug when it is damp for the same reason. Don't use a shirred rug as a scuff mat. The abrasion from shoes and the dirt particles will cut the warp threads.

Basically shirred rugs just need regular vacuuming with the suction attachment (not the rotating carpet beater). Turn over reversible rugs at regular intervals.

Violent rug shaking is not desirable with shirred or standing wool rugs, but they can be draped over a clothesline and "beaten" with an old fashioned rug beater or a clean broom. Occasionally, depending on how heavily the rug is soiled, a wool rug should be hand washed or dry cleaned.

If you have used washable fabrics in the rug, it can be machine washed on the gentle cycle, or hand-washed in the bathtub. Do not put the rug in the washer by itself. Add a sheet or two to keep the rug from being abraded by the agitator. After washing, lay the rug flat to dry. Don't handle a wet rug from the edge. Instead move it as a bundle. If the rug is hung up to dry, the stitching may stretch and the rug will be pulled out of shape.

Hanging Shirred or Standing Wool Rugs for Display

Because these rugs are so showy, they make wonderful wall decorations as well as rugs. The problem is that they really don't cooperate with standard hanging techniques that can be used for such things as hooked rug. The easiest way to hang these is by using small finishing nails to create a support system directly on the wall.

Hold the rug in the desired spot. Use 6d (6 penney) finish nails. Work each nail through the rug in between the fabric strips, and tap the nails into place. Start along the top edge of the rug (about 1/2-inch inside) and set nails every four to six inches. Make another row of nails about six inches lower, and another until you reach the lower edge of the rug. This procedure works best with drywall walls since when you want to move the rug, the tiny holes can be spackled to cover them up.

If you want to hang the rug like a picture, you can use the same nailing system on a backing of wood or a cork bulletin board. (The cork shouldn't be used by itself, it is too flexible to hold the nails. An inexpensive bulletin board is needed for stiffness.)

For rugs with a curved top or irregular shape, you can sew curtain rings to the back, about an inch from the upper edge, spaced about six inches apart. Use a picture-hanging hook or nail to support each ring. This works for small hangings (not more than three square feet). Larger rugs need more support than the rings.

Questions I Get Asked

I enjoy teaching rug making since my students always seem to know just the right questions to ask. These are a sampling of them.

How do I cover up mistakes in stitching?

With the standing wool and sewn center-shirring rugs, it is important to always insert the needle back in the spot in the center of the rug. Beginners sometimes get so interested in the process, they don't quite do it, so there is a small bit of the thread which shows on the surface.

The easiest way to cover mistakes is to use a thread that is lighter in color and/or tone that the fabrics used for the rug. (White and off-white works for everything.) Then if you have a misplaced stitch that shows on the surface, you can just color it to match. Use a permanent marker in a color similar to the fabric and carefully touch up the visible thread.

Remember that rugs, and even wall hangings will generally be seen at a distance, so the fix won't show, and the little bit of exposed thread won't affect the durability of the rug.

Can I Use Wool Blends?

Yes, there are a lot of wool blends and synthetic wool look-alikes that are used for clothing. They will work just fine in shirred rugs and can be used with 100% wools. The old bonded wools should be washed to see if you can peel off the backing fabrics, but if not use them by themselves for a small project.

How Big of a Rug Will a Sweater Make?

Just one women's medium sweater will generally make a good size chairpad (16 to 18 inches), even when the strips are an inch wide. Four sweaters will make a small rug, about two feet by three feet.

Can I Use Cotton Yarn with Cotton Sweaters?

Yes, yarns like the "Sugar 'n Cream" brand can be used to shir and stitch rugs with cotton sweaters. Use a yarn needle or tapestry needle to handle the yarn with sewn center-shirring.

Can I Do Edge Shirring with Recycled Sweaters?

Yes, but the strips will need to be cut wider. You don't want to shir within three lines of knitting from the edge of the strip, so for edge shirring, you want strips that are have not less than eight lines of knitted stitches.

How Do I Make THAT Rug?

When someone sees a finished shirred or beaded rug, they often want to recreate it. The truth is that unless you have the exact fabrics, the rug is going to look different.

For example, the shirred rug on the back cover, with the heathered appearance always generates that question. That particular rug was made from a vintage piece of blanket wool that had bold figures in lots of bright colors and black. The heathering simply comes about from using that type of fabric, and the effect is the same whether it is sewn-center shirred, crocheted with faux shirring, or made with any of the crocheted shirring methods. So, to make that rug, all you have to do is find that kind of fabric.

The real beauty of shirred and standing wool rugs is that there aren't two alike, so the best approach is just to use what you have available and your own creativity to make your own unique rugs.

How Much Can I Sell a Shirred Rug For?

This question is pretty common, and the numbers can be quite startling with these types of rugs. Even 20 years ago, fairly small pictoral, shirred hangings (18" X 24") were selling for $150 to $200 in our rug shops. I've heard recently of a 4-foot diameter rug going for $2,000. These are rugs that are in the "art" category, but shirred rugs are still so little known that even "plain" rugs will sell at the upper end of the rug market. Of course, you have to know your market, so don't try to get those kinds of prices at the church bazaar or farmer's market. But even there, a chairpad from a recycled sweater should fetch $30 or more depending on where you live. And, since many of these techniques are so simple that children can do them, the can be used for raising money for groups. (For more advice, see the article "Making Money, Making Rugs" on the Rugmakers Homestead website.)

Are These Rugs Suitable for Children?

The answer is "yes, if..." and the if has to do with some common sense on the part of the adults involved. Some grade school children will have the fine motor skills for shirring rugs, others will not. If yours do, always make sure they are using a blunt tipped needle. One recent student enjoyed learning beaded wool rugs so much that she taught her youngsters to string the beads, which they loved doing. She then stitched the beads together to form the rug. That sort of shared task is a good approach with younger children. Have them do the simple sewing for shirring or beading and then turn their work over to an adult for assembly.

Older kids can take on some of the more complex assemblies, like the crocheted faux shirring if they have basic crocheting skills. Just don't try to teach them crocheting and rug making at the same time. Even adults have trouble with that.

Are Crochet-Shirred rugs Better than Sewn-Shirred Rugs?

Certainly not. I approach teaching the rugs with the simplest methods presented first, but that is not to say that the more complicated methods are better, or make better rugs. With certain fabrics, crocheted shirring works best since the stitches will space out the folds. But for almost all fabrics, sewn shirring is the fastest and makes wonderful rugs as long as the assembly stitches aren't placed more than 1/2-inch apart. So, just choose a method that appeals to you, there isn't any inherent virtue that makes one technique "better" than another.

Where Can I Find Affordable Wool for Beaded Rugs?

My standard response is to haunt thrift shops for wool coats and blankets, but this student had looked there (in the fall) and found asking prices of $20 and more for coats. So, let me change my advice: haunt the the thrift shops in the spring, when coats get deeply discounted. To make coats into the heavy wool needed to make beaded rugs, wash them in hot water and dry them in a hot dryer. This fulls the coats, shrinking and thickening the wool. Of course, the coat should be made from 100% wool.

Can I Use Lining Material for Shirred Rugs?

Yes, light and flimsy fabrics used for linings and nightgowns can be used for shirring, but they take more work since you will need to shir several layers together to create a rug with any body at all. Cut the strips according to the type of fabric (woven or knitted), and test to see how many layers are needed to make a fold that is at least 1/8-inch across (1/4-inch is better). Sewn center shirring is usually the technique you'll need to use, along with a pointed needle.

Why Should My Rug Lay Flat?

Some years ago, a gal proudly showed me her bent-hook style shirred rug. It was about 30 inches across and was waving like a doily. When I mentioned that that wasn't a good thing, she told me that *her teacher* had told her it was ok, because the rug could be forced flat.

Apparently that piece of advice has been spread around so here is why rugs need to lay flat. First, while small rugs can be forced to flatness, there is a limt. At some point, usually about three feet in diameter, the bulk of the shirred fabric just becomes too much to force flat and if you flatten the rug in one place, it will pop up in another.

Second, rugs get wavy because there are too many stitches in the rounds. Those extra stitches are extra work and they use up extra fabric. So, even if you only look at it from the point of view of making a rug efficiently, a flat rug wins. To keep the crocheted bent-hook rugs laying flat, I developed a reliable pattern for the frequency of "increase" rows, so you don't have to guess any longer about how to "increase as necessary" to keep your rugs laying flat. That information had always been missing from the commercial directions for the various bent hooks.

FIRST BONUS CHAPTER

POSTAGE STAMP RUGS

Even though I've been writing about traditional rag rugs for twenty-five years, something new is always cropping up. One rug technique that I'd never had much use for is the "strung shag" rug. To make them, small bits of fabric were sewn on a string and then the string was knitted or crocheted to make a shaggy rug. Unfortunately, once the shag pieces were worked in, the string had to be broken so more pieces could be strung. In the late 19th century, folks didn't mind too much since they could use up their balls of odd pieces of leftover string. (The backs of many of those old rugs are as colorful as the front sides.)

The process of stopping and starting these rugs with new string was just too time-consuming for my taste, though I did write up the procedure for the knitted version in the first volume of the Rugmaker's Handbooks "*Knitted Rag Rugs for the Craftsman.*" While I was re-writing this book, it dawned on me that the techniques used for crocheted shirring could be adapted to make a crocheted "strung shag" rug much more efficiently.

Instead of stringing small pieces of fabric along a string, they could be threaded onto an afghan hook and then worked off with crochet stitches forming the base of the rug. I was delighted with the improvement of the slow "strung shag" procedure, so I'm including it as a bonus in this book, since it uses the same tools and and a similar technique as the crocheted-shirred rugs. Another great feature of this technique is that it can be used with light quilting cottons.

Postage stamp rugs can be made single-sided or reversible. If you use small squares of fabric and work through the centers, the rug is reversible and not so thick as to be a hazard. If you use longer rectangles of fabric, all of the ends are on the same side resulting in a thicker rug with longer shags, but not reversible.

DIRECTIONS FOR A POSTAGE STAMP RUG

Cut one-inch squares of fabric by first cutting a one inch strip on the bias, then cutting the strip into one inch squares (slightly larger squares are fine for lightweight fabrics).

Insert the tip of a small crochet hook (or afghan hook) into the center of the square. For heavy fabrics like denim, use the pointed end of an afghan hook (see Chapter 8 for appropriate hook sizes and how to use the afghan hook). Put as many squares on the hook as can be handled easily while crocheting.

Base Chain: Use a good quality mercerized crochet cotton thread. Make a slip knot and put it on the end of the hook. Pull one square of fabric off the hook, so that the slip knot comes through it. Chain 2.

Pull off another square and chain 2. Repeat until your base chain is of the desired length. End the chain by pulling off a square of fabric.

First Row: Turn work and chain 1. Skip the space between the first two squares. Insert the hook under the chain stitch between the next two squares and complete a single crochet stitch. *Chain 1, pull off square, chain 1, single crochet in next space*
Repeat the * sequence to the end of the row, ending with pulling off a square of fabric. (Note that this is slightly different than the grid-style of crocheted bent-hook shirring.)

Second and Following Rows: Turn work and chain 1. Skip the space between the first two squares. Insert the hook under the single crochet stitch between the next two squares and complete a single crochet stitch. *Chain 1, pull off square, chain 1, single crochet in next space*
Repeat the * sequence to the end of the row, ending with pulling off a square of fabric.

Continue crocheting rows until the rug reaches the desired size. End the last row by pulling off a square of fabric, chain 1, clip thread at least six inches from the work. Pull end up through last chain to end off. Work the end of the thread back into the rug using an embroidery needle.

Double Crochet Variation
You can replace the single crochet stitches with double crochet stitches if the rug surface is too tight to work easily. In the above directions, you will want to chain 2 everywhere the directions say to chain 1.

Using double crochet, you can also make postage stamp rugs in any of the shapes for the "bent hook" type of crocheted shirring. Just follow the same patterns in Chapter 11.

FOR A SINGLE-SIDED RUG WITH LONG SHAGS
Cut the fabric into strips ¾ inch wide as twice as long as you want the shaggy surface to be. Fold the strips in half lengthwise. Thread the strips onto the crochet hook by inserting the hook just above the folded end (1/4 inch or less from the fold).

Follow the same crochet directions as above, making sure that as you work all of the shag ends stay to the same side.

SECOND BONUS CHAPTER

"CATERPILLAR" RUGS

The "caterpillar" rugs are the oldest form of rag rugs that include shirred strips. The Shakers included these rugs in their catalog and so their history is fairly well known. I decided to include them here since they are so often mis-identified as true "shirred" rugs, and by demonstrating the difference in construction between shirred rugs and caterpillar rugs, it may help to clear up some of the confusion.

Caterpillar rugs were traditionally begun by using light to medium weight wool, but you can make them with just about any fabric that has some resilience, including old sweaters, t-shirts or jeans. Cut strips from the fabrics ¾ to 1 inch wide (see the Handbook section for which direction to cut your particular fabric.)

Use an embroidery needle or other long needle and a doubled thread. This first step is identical to sewn center shirring, so you can use the information in that chapter for appropriate needles and threads for this step.

Shir the length of the strips, in and out, with stitches about ½ inch apart. In contrast to sewn center-shirring, you really want to pack the folds tightly along the string so that the folds twist around it. Knot off the ends of the string securely. These shirred sections are the "caterpillars" and when made properly will be generally round in profile. Note that if you make lots of short caterpillars, you will have more flexibility in creating a design in the rug.

Select a durable base fabric such as cotton duck, denim or mattress ticking. Cut the fabric to the desired size and shape for your rug and hem the edges by folding over to the **front** side of the fabric. (This creates a clean back finish for the rug.)

The caterpillars are handsewn to the base fabric using a modified couching stitch. Use a regular sewing needle and strong thread. Upholstery thread is fine, but the best one is Coats and Clarks Heavy Duty Hand Quilting thread which is a smooth, strong, polyester-cotton blend. The sewing thread is used doubled.

You can begin stitching the caterpillars anywhere on the rug, either in straight rows, in a round or oval spiral or any freeform shape or particular design you have in mind. The first step is to make a stitch back and forth through the end of the caterpillar, securing the knot. Then stitch down through the base fabric which will hold the end of the caterpillar in place.

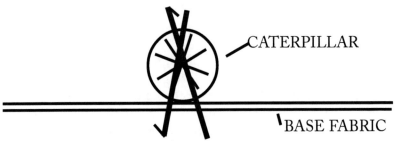

Stitch Up, then Stitch Down,
on either side of the caterpillar

Bring the needle up through the base fabric about ½ inch from the first stitch, and up through the fabric on one side of the caterpillar. Pull up the thread snugly. Insert the needle back into the same spot where the thread emerges, but angle the needle so that it goes down through the opposite side of the caterpillar and then through the base fabric. Pull the thread snug.

If you inserted the needle in the correct spot, the stitch will sink into the caterpillar and be invisible on the front of the rug. The thread should be pulled snug so that the caterpillar is held firmly to the base fabric, but not pulled so tight that it distorts the caterpillar or causes bunching of the base fabric.

For the next stitch, insert the needle about ½ inch away so that it goes up and through the caterpillar again. Pull the thread snug. Insert the point of the needle in the same place that the thread emerges so that it is angled down into the opposite side of the caterpillar and comes out through the base fabric.

The process continues along the length of the caterpillar, until it is entirely stitched to the base. Knot off and rethread the needle as necessary, hiding any knots inside the folds of the caterpillar (not on the back of the rug).

When one caterpillar is completely stitched, begin the next. Each caterpillar should fit solidly up against the previous caterpillar, not simply touching it, but snug up against it. The base fabric should not be visible at all.

Continue adding caterpillars until the rug surface is covered. At the outer edge, the caterpillars should be centered along the folded edge so that the backing fabric cannot be seen.

Caterpillar rugs are light-duty rugs, but can be used in bedrooms or where there isn't a lot of foot traffic. A rug pad is a good idea as it will protect the back stitching from wear. The rugs can be vacuumed (suction only) and hand washed. A second fabric can be used on the back the rug to cover the stitching if desired.

Resources

The Rugmakers Homestead www.rugmakershomestead.com
Information about all types of traditional rug making as well as color photographs of the rugs. Links to current suppliers for rug making tools.

LACIS www.lacis.com
Schirren hooks, needles and threads for shirred rugs.

Shirret www.shirret.com
Shirret(TM) hooks for bent hook crocheted shirring.

National Gallery of Art
www.nga.gov/collection/gallery/iadshake-29277.html
A painting of a Shaker floral motif caterpillar rug with a four-strand braided border

Afterword

In previous handbooks, I have noted that I never really felt that the books were "done." With this book, I know that it is just a beginning. The techniques here simply shine with potential for the textile explorer and fiber artist in all of us. It is my hope that you will take these rugs to new heights.

About the Author

Trained as a wildlife biologist and with long-standing family traditions of textile skills, Mrs. Gray has demonstrated a unique talent for researching and being able to reproduce old rug making techniques. Beginning in the 1970s she also experimented with new textile structures and in the 1980s began writing about rug making. When asked about her purpose in documenting the hundreds of rug making methods, she told the *Idaho Art's Journal* in 1987, "I am the door through which others will walk." Her goal has always been to teach others to make rugs and thereby preserve the methods for future generations. Mrs. Gray lives in the mountains of northern Idaho.

CPSIA information can be obtained at www.ICGtesting.com
Printed in the USA
LVOW132110200912

299579LV00002B/55/P